James Hamilton

The Mount of Olives and other lectures on prayer

James Hamilton

The Mount of Olives and other lectures on prayer

ISBN/EAN: 9783337283902

Printed in Europe, USA, Canada, Australia, Japan

Cover: Foto ©Lupo / pixelio.de

More available books at **www.hansebooks.com**

THE
MOUNT OF OLIVES

AND OTHER

LECTURES ON PRAYER.

BY THE

REV. JAMES HAMILTON,

Author of "Harp on the Willows," "Life in Earnest," "Happy Home," "Royal Preacher," "Lamp and Lantern," "Lady Colquhoun," etc.

NEW-YORK:
ROBERT CARTER & BROTHERS,
530 BROADWAY.
1875.

TO THE

KIRK SESSION AND CONGREGATION

OF THE

NATIONAL SCOTCH CHURCH,

REGENT SQUARE.

My dear Friends.—Of all ministerial employments—and some of them are exceedingly delightful—there is none in which I am so happy, nor so sure that I am profitably engaged, as when meditating over, and writing down, the truths of the Bible for your benefit. These sometimes come out to view with a vividness and beauty which words cannot perpetuate, but still with a radiance which, to my own memory, lingers on many texts, and has left an entrancement round days and places devoted to their study. And just as I rejoice when a day of uninvaded leisure secures some fresh materials for the edification and comfort of that beloved people whose welfare lies nearest my heart; so I have sometimes had to mourn when personal exhaustion, or stormy weather, or some adverse incident on Sabbath, frustrated the meditation of the week. There is the two-fold sadness, that one's thoughts have perished, and that another opportunity of doing good is gone for ever

And yet the mere wish to preserve a fragment of these Saturday musings would not be a sufficient reason for printing them. I feel that something like the following pages is a needful supplement to a tract with which you are already acquainted.* Besetting as the sin of indolence is, we shall find many persons diligent who are not devout. Perhaps some of these may read this little book, and, by the blessing of God, may see prayer in a new light, and be led themselves to practise it.

Except that in the third and seventh Lectures three discourses have been condensed into one, and several have been omitted altogether, I have not made many alterations. I thought it best to retain the sermonic style, as well as the homely illustrations so hazardous in print.

This is not a treatise on prayer. Those who desire something fuller and more systematic will find a variety of excellent works already provided. None is more comprehensive, or more enriched by Scriptural truth, and extensive acquaintance with Christian literature, or by its tone more calculated to awaken devotional feeling, than the well-known treatise of my revered and beloved friend Mr. Bickersteth. I lately read with much pleasure a small volume by Mr M'Gill, of Hightae, " Enter into thy closet." It is judicious, systematic, and practical. For original and elevated sentiment, delicate observation, and experimental wisdom, conveyed in the happiest style, we have few books comparable to Mr Sheppard's " Thoughts on Private Devotion."

I have a friend,—many will know him when I say that his large accomplishments and lofty mind intended

* Life in Earnest.

him for authorship,—but his unweariable benevolence and consummate taste have hitherto kept him busy as the referee and coadjutor of all his book-making acquaintance. When he discovered what I was about, he lent me a manuscript volume of notes of the late Mr. Foster's Lectures,—several of them on the subject of prayer. Had there been room I should have quoted more freely from them, in the hope that their gnarled vigour would lend a strength and solidity to the text; but this book is already too long, and the notes are worthy of being printed separately. And now that I am acknowledging obligations, I cannot refuse to my grateful feelings the satisfaction,—and I hope he will not be angry at it,—of mentioning how much I owe, in the way of suggesting subjects and trains of thought to the conversations of another friend,—one to whose eminent professional talents and personal kindness I owe numberless obligations, and to whom I am indebted for my first acquaintance with more than one field of theological authorship. Amongst others, he induced me to read the writings of Alexander Knox,—an author from whom I have, perhaps, learned the more, all the rather that, in many things, I am constrained to differ from him.

It would have made the course,—such as it is,—more complete, had the Lecture on " Social and United Prayer" been added. The especial blessing attached to consentaneous prayer is one peculiarity of the New Testament dispensation, and its abundant exercise is a delightful token of Christian vitality. This year is likely to be ushered in with a larger amount of united supplications than opened any year since the commencment of the Christian era; and I doubt not this agreement in prayer is the harbinger of better days in the Church's history.

Our own prayer-meeting on Monday evening has often been a season of refreshing. When conducted by our brethren, the elders and deacons, it is the minister's Sabbath, and, like yourselves, I have nothing to do but to worship. And whenever I see a goodly attendance, I am led to hope that the previous day has been a day of profit, and that the remainder of the week will reap the blessing of that prayerful hour.

My beloved hearers, amidst many misgivings occasioned by want of time for revising it, I send this little book to you. I know that you will receive it kindly for the truth's sake and for the author's sake; and, as it is, I am glad to think that you have in this more permanent form, and with all your friendly prepossessions, words which were some of them spoken in weakness, but which, even when dead, I should still desire to speak. Should you derive any profit from perusing them,—" Brethren, pray for us."

Ever most affectionately yours,

JAMES HAMILTON

January 1 1846

CONTENTS.

LECTURE I.

THE MOUNT OF OLIVES.

Mountains of Scripture. Olivet. The Saviour's Compassion. The Agony in Gethsemane. The Saviour's Example in Prayer. Submission. Perseverance. Preparation for suffering. The Saviour's Love to his Own . . . . Page 11

LECTURE II.

THE PARTING PROMISE AND THE PRESENT SAVIOUR

Climbing Plants. The Tree of Life. Reasons why Men do not love the Lord Jesus. The Saviour neither dead, nor distant, nor different from what he was. Christ ever present with his people. His presence sanctifying and sustaining. Paul and Nero. Christ's presence comforting. The Short Journey. Bunyan in Prison, and Rutherford in banishment. The Infant Dreamer. "For ever with the Lord." . . . Page 25

LECTURE III.

THE HEARER OF PRAYER. THE INTERCESSOR ABOVE THE PROMPTER WITHIN.

Prayer has actual Power. The Petitionless Prayer. The Efficacy of Prayer revealed. It is Matter of Fact. *A priori* Objections irrelevant. The Declarations of God himself. The Saviour's Testimony. Instances of answered Prayer. Newton's Experience. The Inhabitant of Jupiter, and the Husbandman. God is the Hearer of Prayer, for he is the Living God, the Almighty, and the God of Love. The Mediation of Christ. The Work of the Spirit. Guilt on the Conscience. Dull Perception. The Dog and the Naturalist. Cold Affections. The Intermitting Fountain. The Disposition to ask Wrong Things, and to ask Right Things in a Wrong Way. . . Page 44

LECTURE IV.

THE PRIVILEGE OF PRAYER.

Athenian Curiosity. A Supposition. Another. Affliction. The Shipwrecked Mariner. Perplexity. Mentor. Solomon's request. The Important undertaking. The Warrior and the broken Buckle. Henry IV. Michael Angelo. The Spiritual Inquirer. The Blind Man of Bethsaida . . . Page 70

CONTENTS　ix

LECTURE V.

THE OPEN REWARD OF SECRET PRAYER

The Closet. Abraham. Isaac. David. Cornelius. John Welsh. Peden The stated Place. The secret Reward. Jacob at Jabbok. The Talisman. Presence of Mind. Nehemiah. Boerhaave. Spirituality. The Smell of the Ivory Palace. The open Reward of the great Day. Prayers self-registering . . . Page 80

LECTURE VI.

REASONS WHY PRAYER IS NOT ANSWERED.

The blank Petition. The wrong Channel. The Serpent asked. The wrong Motive. The Prayer countermanded by the contrary Sir.. Unbelief. The Answer comes unawares . . . Page 104

LECTURE VII

CONFESSION, ADORATION, AND THANKSGIVING.

Confession. Remorse and Silence. The Psalmist. Sullenness. Callousness The Fountain opened. The Scape-Goat.—*Adoration*. The bestowment of the Affections. Platonism. Mysticism. Asceticism. Christianity. Refuge and Solace in the Divine Perfections.—*Thanksgiving* Interpositions. The best Gifts. Joseph Alleine. The joyful Life . . . . Page 114

LECTURE VIII

BIBLE INSTANCES.

History. Enoch. Moses. David. Matthew. Henry Cornelius Winter. Bishop Heber. Dr. Williams. Count Zinzendorf. S. Pearce. President Edwards. Daniel. A Praying Atmosphere. The Diving Water Spider   **Page 134**

LECTURE IX.

CONCLUSION.

What is Prayer? Communion with God. Peace and Joy. Exotic blessings. The Branch running over the Wall. Intercession. M. J. Grahame   **Page 149**

LECTURE I.

THE MOUNT OF OLIVES.

"And he went, as he was wont, to the Mount of Olives."—LUKE xxii. 39.

THE mountains are Nature's monuments. Like the islands they dwell apart, and like them they give asylum from a noisy and irreverent world. Many a meditative spirit has found in their silence leisure for the longest thought, and in their Patmos-like seclusion the brightest visions and largest projects have evolved; whilst by a sort of over-mastering attraction, they have usually drawn to themselves the most memorable incidents which variegate our human history. And, as they are the natural haunts of the highest spirits, and the appropriate scenes of the most signal occurrences, so they are the noblest cenotaphs. Afar off they arrest the eye; and though their hoary chronicle tells its legend of the past, their heaven-pointing elevations convey the spirit onward towards eternity. We do not wonder that excited fancy has sought relics of the ark on the top of ARARAT, and in the grim solitude of SINAI it is solemn to remember and easy to believe that the voice of Jehovah has spoken here.

Elijah has made Carmel all his own, and the death of Moses must be ever Pisgah's diadem. The words of Jesus seem still to linger on the hills of Galilee, their lilies forbidding " thought for raiment," and their twittering little birds " no thought for to-morrow," whilst every grassy tuft and scented flower is breathing its own beatitude. But though heavenly wisdom spake on that mountain-side, and excellent glory lighted up the top of Tabor, there is another height to which discipleship reverts with fonder memory, and which it treads with softer step—that mountain where beyond any spot in Palestine " God was manifest in flesh"—where the great Intercessor was wont to pray, where Jesus wept over Jerusalem, on whose slopes he blessed the Apostle-band, and sent his message of mercy to mankind —the mountain at whose base lay Bethany and Gethsemane—on whose gentle turf his feet last stood, and where they yet may stand again—the Sabbatic, pensive, and expectant Mount of Olives.

Round this Incarnation-monument let our thoughts this day revolve. To learn the mind which was in Christ, and so the mind which is in God, let us confine our view to that little spot and ponder those scenes in the Saviour's history and those words in the Saviour's ministry of which the theatre was Olivet. And whilst we do this for purposes of general piety, to get materials for our faith and love, let us, as the best introduction to a few discourses on Prayer, keep an especial eye to the suppliant Saviour. That we may know the Intercessor above, there is no way so excellent as to get acquainted with that same Jesus while he sojourned here below.

1. Olivet reminds us of the Saviour's pity for such as perish. It was a pleasant evening in spring, and the Holy Land looked happy. The rapid verdure—the bright blush of the pomegranate, and the tender scent of the budding vines—the nestling dove in her murmuring joy, and the colt and lamb in their crazy gambols—all felt the gush of vernal glee. And people felt it. It was the sundy paschal tide, and the waysides resounded with shouting pilgrims on their journey to Jerusalem. From Hermon to Zion it was one long stream of music and merry hearts, and even round the Man of Sorrows it looked like a dawn of joy. They seem at last to guess his mission and suspect his glory. They are conducting him in triumph. They are rending down the palm-branches and cleaving the welkin with their shouts, "Hosannah to the Son of David," and proud is he on whose mantle the pacing colt of their new monarch sets his elated foot.—But why this solemn pause? this slackened gait, this quivering lip, this tearful eye? Jerusalem is full in sight—straight over yon narrow vale, so near that you may count each stone of the glistening temple, and catch from the teeming streets this evening's tune of mingled gladness. Is it not a goodly sight? yon gorgeous fane, the true Jehovah's sanctuary, yon crowding population—God's ancient people—and more than all, the thought of happy meetings and blessed homes on which this evening's sun will set? But the Saviour saw another crowd, and heard another shout.

Through the darkened noon he saw the erected cross, and round it heard the frantic mob exclaiming, "Away with him, away with him—Crucify him, crucify him—His blood be on us and our children." The Saviour saw another sight. Across the gulf of forty years he looked as clearly as then he looked across the valley of Jehoshaphat, and saw the dismal prayer fulfilled. He saw another passover, and another multitude, and another evening like this—but saw that there should never be the like again. He beheld the Roman eagle swoop down on his quarry, and in the straitness of that siege saw things from which the piteous soul of Immanuel shrunk away. He saw another sight. He saw these goodly stones all tumbled down, and barley growing in silent fields where now so many footsteps nimbly tripped it—no temple, no ephod, no priest, no passover. And, oh! he saw yet another sight. He saw another world, and in its sullen gloom and endless weeping recognized many a one whose beaming face and sparkling eye lit up that evening's festival. As if already in the place of woe he looked on many round him; and though their voices were that moment merry and shouting in his train, he knew that they would despise his blood and hate his Heavenly Father, and their present mirth made Jesus weep the more. "He beheld the city, and wept over it, saying, If thou hadst known, even thou, in this thy day, the things which belong unto thy peace! but now they are hid from thine eyes."

Every tear that Jesus wept is a mystery, and this solemn incident in the Redeemer's history no one can entirely explain. But, my dear friends, it teaches this awful lesson—that some may share a Saviour's tears who never profit by a Saviour's blood. It shows that his pity for sinners is far beyond their pity for themselves O Christless sinner! these tears of the Saviour speak to thee. They ask, Do you know to what a hell you are going, and what a heaven you are losing? You may be merry now—but so was Jerusalem then—and yet its mirth made Jesus weep the more. You may be light-hearted and lovely to your friends—and so were many of those whose ungodly souls and dark hereafter made Jesus weep. You may be in the midst of mercy and surrounded with the means of grace —and so were they; but mercy so near them and grace rejected only made the Saviour's tears flow faster. "Would that thou hadst known in this thy day, the things that belong to thy peace." And you may have even some interest about the Saviour. Under some erroneous impression, or on a holiday triumph, you may join the jubilant company and shout Hosannah—but oh! if you despise his blood or join the world that crucifies him, you are one of those whose cup of wrath will only be embittered by a pitying Saviour's slighted tears. You who never come to a communion—you who have never got such faith in a dying Saviour, or such love to him as to do this in remembrance of him—you who do nothing to identify yourselves with the Nazarene— the Crucified,—whose zeal is all expended on the road from Jericho to Jerusalem—who never follow to the guest-chamber, to Gethsemane, to the cross, to the tomb and back into a scorning world—you who are not moved by a Saviour's blood, will you not be melted by a Saviour's tear? That tear fell from an eye which had looked into eternity, and knew the worth of souls. It fell from an eye which was not used to weep for nothing, and which must have seen something very sad before it wept at all. It fell from an eye which, O sinner! would glisten with ecstasy if it saw thy dry lids moistening and thy dry heart melting—an eye which would sparkle in affection over thee if it saw thee weeping for thyself, and weeping for the pierced One.

2. The Mount of Olives reminds us of the Redeemer's *agony to save*. At the foot of the mountain, and between two paths, both of which lead over the hill to Bethany, is a little enclosure called Gethsemane.* To this day it contains some singularly large and very ancient olive-trees. Being on the way-side to Bethany, and at a convenient distance from the noise and interruption of Jerusalem, "Jesus ofttimes resorted thither with his disciples;" and when he crossed the brook and got in, either alone or with his little company, under the soft shelter of the olive branches, and the city gates were closed, and no footfall was heard on either path, he enjoyed 'communion high and sweet" with his Heavenly Father. And this holy fellowship endeared the place. It was not the dewy stillness—though that was welcome at the close of the jaded day,—nor the sweet moonlight, and the

---

* See Narrative of a Mission to the Jews, by Messrs Bonar and M'Cheyne, chap. 3.

gentle fall of tiny flakes from the blossoming trees, and the murmur of the brook, and the song of evening birds—though, after the rough jeering and blasphemy of men, the inarticulate music of the loyal universe was thrice welcome to the Saviour's ear; but because in that seclusion He and the Father were alone together. Intercourse such as he enjoyed while as yet in the Father's bosom he tasted here, and it so gladdened and strengthened his soul that he ofttimes resorted thither. Others would go home to sleep, but Jesus would go here to pray. Every man went, at evening, to his own place; but Jesus "went to the Mount of Olives."* And, as it had been the scene of his highest delights, he selected it as the fittest place for his deepest sorrow. The Son of Man had no dwelling of his own; but Gethsemane was the Saviour's "closet."* It was there that, in secret, he had so often prayed to his Father; and as the memory of blessed moments, and the sunshine of heaven opened, rested on it, now that grief was near, he, as it were, entered into it and shut to the door. But oh! how changed! 'Tis no longer the same Gethsemane. All his days of flesh the Surety had been bearing his people's sin, and at all times carrying in his bosom the vial of indignation due to their sin. But it was not wrath poured out, it was wrath in a vial. Now, however, the vial burst, and his inmost soul was drenched in its burning fury. He was sore amazed. To be made "a curse" was a new thing to Immanuel. To be brought into such

* John vii 53; viii 1   * Matt. vi. 6.

horrid contact with the thing which his soul hated—to be numbered with transgressors, and to bear the sin of many—was a strange and appalling thing to the Holy One of God. He was sore amazed! A cup was put into his harmless hand; and, as he gazed at this cup of trembling, it was not the sharp anguish of the flesh, nor the taunts of ruffian men, nor the malignity of hideous fiends,—but it was guilt which made its bitter dregs and the Father's wrath its flaming overflow. And though his hand was too gentle and filial to fling that cup away, separateness from sin, and the joyful sense of his Father's love, were to Jesus dearer than life; and though his omnipotent hand still clasped the cup, his holy soul revolted from it, and in ecstasy of pain —in the agony of a bloody sweat—he prayed that it might pass from *him*. But had *he* not drunk it, that cup must have journeyed on, and all his people, in a lost eternity, must have drunk it for themselves; and though the fainting flesh prompted him to let it pass, and the hatred of the accursed thing, and the instinct after the Father's smile, seconded the prayer of the feeble flesh, love to man still held it fast, and love to the Father enabled him to drink it all. And when at last, from its paroxysm of woe, he wakened up in the strengthening angel's arms, the work was well-nigh done, justice was all but satisfied, and the Church all but saved; and, for the joy so much nearer now, the cross had no error and the sepulchre no gloom; and, now that the bitterness of death was past, Judas and his torch-lit band could not come too quickly.

Oh, what wonders love hath done!
  But how little understood!
God well knows, and God alone,
  What produc'd that sweat of blood:
Who can thy deep wonders see,
Wonderful Gethsemane!

There my God bore all my guilt:
  This through grace can be believed:
But the horrors which he felt,
  Are too vast to be conceived:
None can penetrate through thee,
Doleful, dark Gethsemane!*

3. The Mount of Olives is identified with the supplications and intercessions of Immanuel, and so suggests to us the Lord Jesus as *the great example in prayer*. The supplications which ascended on those solitary nights, when, of his people, there was none with him, survive in no human record; yet, doubtless, to the end of time our world will be indebted to the lonely hours when the Man of Sorrows watched and prayed upon the Mount of Olives. The petitions offered in Gethsemane the pen of Inspiration has preserved; and the seventeenth of John records a long and fervent prayer offered, in all likelihood, in some calm spot near the same venerable mountain's base. In these supplications the heavenly High Priest was not only his people's mediator and intercessor, but their model and their guide. And from these we learn—

(1.) Submission in prayer. In praying for his people, the Mediator's prayer was absolute: "Father, *I will.*" But in praying for himself

* Hart's Hymns.

how altered was the language! "Father, if it be possible, let this cup pass from me: nevertheless, not as I will, but as thou wilt.' "Now is my soul troubled, and what shall I say? Father, save me from this hour; but for this cause came I unto this hour. Father, glorify thy name"

(2.) Perseverance in prayer. The Evangelist* tells that there was one prayer which Jesus offered three times, and from the Epistle to the Hebrews we find that this prayer prevailed.† Although the more palpable sufferings did not pass away, the more exquisite and inward anguish, which made his soul exceeding sorrowful even unto death, did pass away. In answer to his "strong crying and tears," he was saved from this deadly and soul-crushing grief.

(3.) The best preparation for trial is habitual prayer. Long before it became the scene of his agony, Gethsemane had been the Saviour's oratory. "He ofttimes resorted thither." But when the hour of darkness came, and he trod the wine-press alone, he found that even *He* had not been there too often. And, brethren, it will be the best preparation for your own days of darkness and scenes of trial, to resort ofttimes thither in anticipatory prayer. Days of bodily weakness or sad bereavement will come abated, and the day of death will come less startling, if in prayer you have oft repaired to it beforehand, and bespoken almighty help against its time of need.

4. The Mount of Olives recalls to us the Saviour's *affection for his own*. I fear that the

* Matt. xxvi. 44. † Heb. v. 7.

love of Christ is little credited even by those who have some faith in his finished work, and some attachment to his living person. There are several relations which link souls on earth together, and the affection, the instinct of endearment created by that relation is in some instances intensely strong; but, O disciple! do you believe that your Saviour's love is stronger? A brother knows how he loves his brother—but their love to one another will not explain a Saviour's love to them—for Jesus is "a friend who sticketh closer than a brother;" a friend whose love will stand severer shocks and enter into finer feelings. A mother knows how she loves the infant in her arms, how little she would grudge the hours spent in watching his feverish slumber, and the health she lost in restoring his; but that will not tell her how a Saviour loves his own. She may forget, but Jesus will not forget his ransomed. And in regard to the most sacred of all relations the Bible says, "Husbands, love your wives even as Christ also loved the Church, and gave himself for it, that he might sanctify it." Not that it is possible to have the same high and self-devoting and transforming love; but the nearer approach to it the nearer a perfect affection. But though the Word of God employs these three comparisons to shadow forth the Saviour's feeling towards his own, the labouring words and disappointed metaphors leave us to infer that there is something in the heart of Immanuel towards his people—something more specific—more solicitous—more bent on their happiness and more bound up in their holiness—more tender and more transforming than anything which the dim affections and drossy emotions of earth can rightly represent. Oh, disciple! do you credit this? Have you not been rather wont to regard yourself as occupying in the Saviour's mind such a place as a star in the firmament, or a symbol in a formula, or a leaf in the forest, or at best a sheep in the uncounted fold? If these be your notions go back to Olivet. Hear the Divine Intercessor at its foot exclaiming, " Neither pray I for these alone, but for all who shall hereafter believe through their word ;" and hear him promising, ere his feet sunder from its grassy slopes, " And lo, I am with you alway, even to the end of the world ;" and recollect that he who prayed thus and who promised thus is He to whom " all power is given in heaven and in earth "—the Alpha and Omega, who is, and was, and is to come—the Almighty. Remember that in his comprehensive eye you as truly had a place as Peter and John, and in his all-sufficient love you have a place as specific if not as large as they. You are one of those over whom he stretched his uplifted hands, and pronounced his parting blessing. You are one of those to whom he has promised another Comforter, and whom he has engaged to be with alway; and though formal teaching may forget it, and your own cold heart may contradict it, if you belong to Christ at all, however much you may be prized and cherished by some around you, there is One unseen who loves you more, and who having loved you from the first will love you to the end.

Except his bodily absence, there is no alteration in the Friend of Sinners. It was ineffable love to the souls of men that brought him to the manger, and that love was nothing less when he hasted to Jerusalem, impatient for the cross. The bloody sweat of Gethsemane did not exhaust that love—the desertion of disciples did not damp it, and the soldiers' buffeting and the rabble's shouts did not disgust it. It was love to men, which in the ransomed thief for a moment brightened his dying hour, which gave him breath to cry, "Father, forgive them," and strength to bow the head and give up the ghost. Love to man was the last thing which left the heart of Jesus, and the first thing that throbbed in it when it was a living heart again. The darkness of Golgotha had not eclipsed it, nor in Joseph's sepulchre had the tomb-damp tarnished it. No sooner was he risen indeed, than this love glowed again so fervent that that resurrection evening it made two faithful hearts on their way to Emmaus burn within them, and after lighting up one little company after another for forty days, in a burst of concentrated kindness, in a blaze of final blessing it vanished from them into heaven. And in the same manner as they saw him go, we shall see him come; the same mighty yet benignant Saviour, as full of grace when he returns the Man of Joys as when he first and for ever ceased to be the Man of Sorrows. And, oh! brethren, do you learn it—do you believe it. Let the Mount of Olives be your incarnation monument. Let the road from Jericho be the record of a Saviour's pity. Let Gethsemane be the measure of a Saviour's desire for souls, and let Bethany be the token how much he loves his own; and like the men of Galilee, let the last and habitual aspect of the Saviour be that look which lingered on their memory till one by one they passed away to see him as he is—that look which spake more love than even his melodious blessing, and which, after the cloud had closed him from the view, made them loath to quit the Mount of Olives.

LECTURE II.

THE PARTING PROMISE, AND THE PRESENT SAVIOUR.

" **And,** lo, I am with you alway, even unto the end of the world."—MATT. xxviii. 20.

There are some plants which grow right up --erect in their own sturdy self-sufficiency, and there are some feeble ones which take hold with their hands and clasp and climb. The soul of man is like these last. Even in his best estate he was not meant to grow insulated and stand alone. He is not strong enough for that. He has not within himself resources sufficient to fill himself. He is not fit to be his own all-in-all. The make of his mind is an out-going, exploring, petitionary make. The soul of man is a clasping, clinging soul, seeking to something over which it can spread itself, and by means of which it can support itself. And just as in a neglected garden you may see the poor creepers making shift to sustain themselves as best they can; one convolvolus twisting round another, and both draggling on the ground; a clematis leaning on the door which will bye and bye open and let the whole mass fall down; a vine or a passion-flower wreathing round a prop which all the while is poisoning it; so in this fallen world it is mournful to see the efforts which human souls are making to get some efficient object to lean upon and twine around. One clasps a glittering prop, and it poisons him. The love of money blasts his soul, and it hangs round its self-chosen stay a blighted, withered thing. Another spreads himself more amply over a broad surface of creature-comfort,—a snug dwelling, and a well-furnished library, and a pleasant neighbourhood, with the command of everything that heart can wish, and a steady income buy,—but death opens the door and, with nothing but vacancy to lean upon, he falls over on the other side all helpless and dejected. And a still greater number, groping about along the ground, clutch to one another, and intertwine their tendrils mutually, and by forming friendships and congenial intimacies, and close relations, try to satisfy their leaning loving nature in this way. But it answers little end. The make of man's soul is upward, and one climber cannot lift another off the ground. And the growth of man's soul is luxuriant, and that growth must be stifled, checked and scanty, if he have no larger space over which to diffuse his aspirations, his affections, and his efforts, than the surface of a fellow-creature's soul. But, weedy as this world-garden is, the Tree of Life still grows in the midst of it,—erect in his own omnipotent self-sufficiency, and inviting every weary straggling soul to lay hold of his everlasting strength, and expatiate upwards along the infinite ramifications of his endless excellencies and all-inviting love.

God has formed the soul of man of a leaning, dependant make; and for the healthy growth and joyful development of that soul, it is essential that he should have some object far higher and nobler than himself to dispread his desires and delights upon. That object is revealed in the Gospel. That object is Immanuel. His divinity is the Almighty prop—able to sustain the adhering soul, so that it shall never perish nor come into condemnation—the omnipotent support which bears the clinging spirit loftily and securely, so that the whirling temptations which vex it cannot rend it from the Tree of Life, and that the muddy plash, which soils and beats into the earth its sprawling neighbours, cannot tarnish the verdant serenity and limpid glories of its flowering head. And just as his divine strength is the omnipotent prop of the adhering soul, so his divine resources and his human sympathy make him the all-sufficient object, over which each emotion and each desire of regenerate humanity may boundlessly diffuse itself. And however delicate your feelings, however eager your affections, and however multitudinous the necessities of your intricate nature, there is that in this Heavenly Friend which meets them every one There are in his unimaginable compassions, and in his benignant fellow-feelings, holds sufficient for every craving tendril and eager clasper of the human heart, to fix upon and wreath around.

This is what the Gospel does. It just offers you a friend, who can both save and satisfy your soul. Jesus, the Son of God, God manifest in flesh, Immanuel, the Gospel offers this Friend to you—not more tender than he is holy, not more divine than he is human. Instead of clutching to props which cannot elevate you, or if they do bear you up for a moment, must soon be withdrawn again,—the Gospel bids you grow against the Tree of Life, and just as you grow up into Christ, you will grow up into holiness and into happiness. And if you have not yet found an object to your heart's content,—if you feel that there is still something wrong with you,—that you are neither leading the life which you would like to lead, nor enjoying the comfort which you think might be somehow got; be advised. Take the Lord Jesus for your friend. He is one in whom you will find no flaw. He is one of whom, —if you really get acquainted with him,—you will never weary; and one, who, if once you really go to Him, will never weary of you. He is a friend of whom no one had ever reason to complain—a friend who has done so much for you already, that he would have done enough even though he were never to do any more, but who is so generous, that his thoughts are all occupied with the great things he designs to do,— a friend who is singularly kind and considerate, for " he sticketh closer than a brother,"—a friend who does not vary, " for he is the same yesterday, to-day, and for ever,"—and, best of all, a friend who is never far away, for " Lo, I am with you alway."

My dear friends,—There are many reasons why men do not love the Lord Jesus. Some feel no need of him. They understand that he is a Saviour: but a Saviour is what they do not desire. Others have no congeniality with him. They understand that his character is divine—that his love of holiness is as intense as his hatred of iniquity,—and as they love the world, and love their own way, and love the pleasures of sin, they feel that they cannot love the Lord Jesus. But the hearts of some towards Christ are cold for other reasons. Their conceptions regarding him are sufficiently vague and dim; but so far as they can be reduced to anything definite, we might say that they do not love the Lord Jesus, because they habitually think of Him as a dead Saviour, or a Saviour different from what he was, or a distant Saviour—a Saviour far away.

I. Some look on the Lord Jesus as dead. They read his history as of one who lived long ago, but who is not living now. They read Matthew's narrative, or John's, and they are interested—for the moment moved. They feel that these words are very beautiful—that this stroke of kindness or tenderness was very touching—that that interposition was very surprising. They feel that the whole history of Jesus of Nazareth is very affecting; and, just as they may have wept at the death of Socrates, or when they read the martyrdom of the saints at Lyons, so they may have felt for him who had not the fox's hole—they may have wept when they saw the son of Mary hanging on the tree. And, if they were visiting Palestine, they might linger over many a silent spot with a solemn impression. "Is this the grassy mount where he preached that sermon? Yon lake, rippling round its pebbly margin, is it the one he so often crossed? and are these the very rocks which echoed the strong crying of his midnight prayers?" But there they feel as if it ended. They look on it all as a tale that is past. They take for granted that it all closed on Calvary—that the cross was the conclusion of that life—the most wonderful life that the world ever saw—but still its conclusion. To them Christ is dead, not living; and therefore no wonder that they do not love him. You may revere the character of those long ago departed; but love is an affection reserved for the living. You will only love the Lord Jesus when you come to believe in him as a living Saviour—one who once was dead, but who, once dead, dieth no more. Jesus lives. He was not more alive when he sat at Jacob's well than he is alive this moment. He was not more alive when he poured the water into the basin and washed their feet—not more alive when he took the cup and made a beginning of the Remembrance-feast—not more alive when he rose from table and sang the parting hymn, and went out among them to the Mount of Olives, than he is living now. The Lord Jesus lives. He is alive for evermore.

II. Some do not love the Lord Jesus because they look on him as an altered Saviour—as different now from what he once was. Earthly friends are apt to change, and if they do not change, they die. When a visitor comes from a foreign land where you once sojourned, you ask eagerly about the different acquaintances you once had there. "And did you see such a one?" "Yes; but you would not know him, he is so greatly altered." "Did he remember me?" "Well, I rather think he was asking for you, but I cannot be very sure. He has got other things to occupy his thoughts since you and he were wont to meet." "And what of such another?" " Ah, times are sadly changed with him. You would be sorry to see him now. I believe he has the same kind heart as ever; but he has not in his power to show it as he used to do." "And our old neighbour, who lived next door?" " Your old neighbour? dear good man, he is safe in Abraham's bosom. I found his house shut up, and all his family gone away." And it is very seldom, after years of absence, that you hear of one whose outward circumstances are nowise different from what they were, and rarer still to hear of one whose dispositions are quite unchanged.

However, One there is who wears our nature, but is not liable to the variations of mortality. ' Jesus Christ is the same yesterday, to-day, and for ever." The concurring testimony of those who have seen him from time to time, along a reach of some thousand years, goes to prove that the Alpha and Omega, the friend of sinners, cannot change. He who talked with our first parents in the cool of the day is the same holy yet condescending one that he ever was, and loveth righteousness, and hateth iniquity, as much as when the first sinners ran away from his pure and sin-repelling presence. The heavenly high priest is still as accessible to prayer, and as ready to yield to his people's entreaty, as when he six times conceded to Abraham's intercession. The God of Bethel is still the faithful keeper of his people and their families as when he heard Jacob in the day of his distress, and was with him in the way which he went.* And anything which has been heard of him since he went back to his glory, goes to prove that he is the same Saviour now as during the continuous years he sojourned with us.

It is true, there are some circumstantial differences, but no intrinsic change. There is more of the oil of gladness on him than when the Father first anointed him, and crowns are on his head which have been planted there since the work given him to do was finished. His satisfactions are fuller, as he continues to see the travail of his soul; and, doubtless, there are outbursts of his glory yet to come, more dazzling than any which have yet astonished heaven. But still the mind of the Lord Jesus is the same as it ever was; and when the last saint sits down beside him on his throne—when the fulness of " It is finished " comes to be understood, and word is brought to the many mansions that death is dead, and that time is now no more—the redeemed, as they bow beneath that exceeding glory, will feel that it is still the glory of the Lamb that was slain—the glory of the friend who sticketh closer than a brother.

III. But the feelings of others towards the Lord Jesus are vague and comfortless, because they think of him as a distant Saviour—a Saviour far away. The Lord Jesus is omnipresent. He is not far from any one of us. His flame-bright eye follows the Sabbath-breaker through the fields, and is on the drunkard as he reels into

* Gen. xxxv 3.

the tavern. It reads the thought of the liar as he forges his falsehood, and looks through and through that heart which is full of its corrupt imaginings. It notices the worldly professor at the communion-table, and sees the unbeliever tumbling, night after night, into his prayerless bed. But though the Lord Jesus be everywhere present, he is present with his own people in a peculiar relation. He is with them as a Saviour, a shepherd, a friend. His divine presence fills immensity; but his gracious and reconciled presence—his loving and interested presence—his Saviour-presence—is exclusively with his own. So constantly is the Lord Jesus present with his people that, in order to get the full good of it, they have only to remember the fact. From the moment that a man becomes a disciple of Christ, "Lo, I am with you alway" becomes a promise to that man—a promise, the performance of which is never for a moment suspended by the Saviour, but the existence of which is often forgot by the disciple. But, forgotten or remembered, it is every moment true; and, to enjoy the full blessedness of this assurance you have only to remember, to realize it. Sometimes, without any effort on your part, the conviction will dawn gently or flash brightly, on the mind, and you will feel for a moment that Jesus is with you. But why not feel it alway? for it is always equally true.

> A glance from heaven, with sweet effect,
> Sometimes my pensive spirit cheers;
> But ere I can my thoughts collect,
> As suddenly it d sappears.

> So lightning in the gloom of night
>   Affords a momentary day;
> Disclosing objects full in sight,
>   Which, soon as seen, are snatch'd away
>
> The lightning's flash did not create
>   The opening prospect it reveal'd;
> But only show'd the real state
>   Of what the darkness had conceal'd.*

These lightning-bursts, these momentary gleams, are just the hints of truth which the Holy Spirit darts into the mind from time to time, revealing matters as they really are. But we ought to recollect, that even during the dark the solid landscape has not vanished, but is only hid. And even so, when Christ's sensible presence is withdrawn, we should remember that he is near as ever, and it is the believer's wisdom to go on in the joyful strength of the assurance, "Lo, I am with you."

Let me mention some benefits of Christ's perpetual presence with his people, especially when that presence is recollected and realized.

1. It is sanctifying. The company of an earthly friend is often influential on character. If he be one of a very pure and lofty mind, and, withal, one who has gained an ascendancy over your own soul, his very presence is a talisman. If an angry storm be gathering in your bosom or lowering in your countenance, the unexpected sunshine of his heavenly aspect will disperse it all again. If mean or unworthy thoughts were creeping into your mind, the interruption of his noble presence will chase them all away. If you are on the

---

* Newton.

point of declining some difficult enterprise or evading some incumbent duty, the glance of his remonstrating eye will at once shame away your indolence or cowardice, and make you up and doing. So the Saviour's recollected presence is a constant reproof and a ceaseless incentive to an affectionate disciple. Is he provoked? Is his temper ruffled? Is he about to come out with some sharp or cutting sarcasm, or to deal the indignant blow? One look from the Lamb of God will calm his spirit—will cool the flush of fury in his burning cheek—will make his swelling heart beat softly. Are you tempted? Do evil thoughts arise in your heart? One glance from these holy eyes can chase away a whole legion of devils, and banish back into the pit each foul suggestion. Are you seized with a lazy or selfish fit? Are you wearying of work which for some time you were doing, or refusing work which God is now giving you to do? Are you angry at an affliction, or averse to a given task? Lo! he puts to his hand and offers to help you with this cross, and you observe that it is a pierced hand; and he offers to go before and show you the way, and you notice that the footprints are bleeding, and it wounds you to think that you should have needed such an admonition. Or you have just come away from a scene of guilt—from a company where you have denied him—where you have just been saying by your conduct, by your silence, or your words, "I know not the man;" and as you encounter the eye of Jesus, whom they are leading away to crucify, O Peter, do you not go forth and weep bitterly!

2. Christ's presence is sustaining. The Apostles were wonderfully calm and collected men. People, considering that they were, many of them, unlearned and ignorant, were amazed at their dignified composure in most difficult circumstances. It was scarcely possible to alarm or agitate them. When brought before kings and rulers, it was usually their judges who trembled, but they themselves were tranquil. And Paul tells us the secret of it. When he himself was brought before Cæsar, it was an agitating occasion. Nero was a cruel prince, and the people looked on his palace much as they would have looked on a leopard's den. An order has arrived to bring the Gallilean prisoner to the emperor's judgment-hall. The Apostle had just time to warn a few friends, and like enough they came and condoled with him; but they thought it prudent not to go with him into court. It might compromise their own safety, and it could do him no effectual good;—and he did not urge them. The soldiers arrived, and he went away cheerily with them—the old weather-beaten man—without his cloak, for he had left it at Troas; without his friends, for he had left them behind at his own hired house—as forlorn as ever prisoner stood before Cæsar. And how was it that the infirm old man passed, with so serene a look, the clashing swords and scowling sentries at the palace-front? How was it that he trod the gloomy gateway with a step so full of merry innocence and martyr-zeal, and never noticed Nero's lions snuffling and howling in their hungry den? And how was it that in the dim and dangerous

presence-chamber, where cruelty sat upon the throne of luxury,—how was it that, with that wolf upon the judgment-seat and those bloodhounds all around him—with none but pagans present, and not one believing friend to bear thee company—how was it, O Paul! that in such an hour of peril, instead of pleading not guilty, and falling down on suppliant knees, thou didst commit the very crime they charged against thee— the crime of loyalty to Jesus—and urge Christ's claims on Cæsar? Why the secret of this strange courage was, "At my first answer no man stood with me, but all forsook me. Notwithstanding, THE LORD stood with me and strengthened me, that by me the preaching might be fully known, and that all the Gentiles might hear; and I was delivered out of the mouth of the lion."

And you, my friends, will all be brought into agitating circumstances. It is not likely that it will be said to you, "Fear not, for thou must stand before Cæsar." But you may be arraigned before terrible tribunals—the tribunal of public opinion—the tribunal of private affection—the tribunal of worldly interest—for Christ's name's sake. From time to time you may be constrained to pass through ordeals which will make you understand how Paul felt when passing in at the palace-gate. When called to give your testimony for Christ, the flesh may be weak, and the willing word may be like to expire in your choking utterance. Wordly wisdom may beckon you back, and, like Paul's fearful friends, cautious or carnal Christians may refuse to support you It is not Nero's hall, but a quiet parlour you are entering; but before you come out again you may be a poor man, or a friendless one. The *Yes* or *No* of one faithful moment may have spurned the ladder of promotion from under your feet, and dashed your brightest hopes on this side the grave. Or, by the time the letter you are now penning is closed and sealed and posted, and the sinful assent, or the compromising proposal, or the resolute refusal is written, the Lord Jesus will have said, "I know thy works, that thou hast a name that thou livest and art dead;" or, "I know thy works, that thou art neither cold nor hot;" or, "I know thy works; behold, I have set before thee an open door, and no man can shut it; for thou hast a little strength, and hast kept my word, and hast not denied my name. I also will keep thee." In such fiery trials of love and fidelity, there is nothing so sure to overcome as the recollected presence of "Lo! I am with you." And oh! it is sweeter, like the three holy children, to pace up and down beneath the furnace' flaming vault, arm in arm with the Son of Man, than to tread the green pastures of an earthly promotion or a carnal tranquillity purchased by the denial of Jesus, and so with the wrath of the Lamb.

3. Comforting. You have noticed the difference in travelling the same road solitary and in pleasant company. "What! we are not here already! It takes three hours to do it, and we have not been half that time. Well, I could not have believed it; but then I never before travelled it with you." No doubt Cleopas and his

comrade used to think the road from Jerusalem to Emmaus long enough, and were very glad when they reached the fiftieth furlong. But that evening when the stranger from Jerusalem joined them, they grudged every waymark which they passed; and as in the progress of his expositions Moses and all the prophets beamed with light from heaven, and their own hearts glowed warmer and warmer, they would fain have counted the mile-stones back again. "How vexing! This is Emmaus; but you must not go on. 'Abide with us, for the day is far spent.'" Any road which you travel solitary is long enough, and any stage of life's journey where no one is with you, will be dreary and desolate. But you need have no such companionless stages—no such cheerless journeys. If you be a disciple, the Lord Jesus always is with you. And whether they be the silent weeks which you spend in search of health in some far away and stranger-looking place, or the long voyage in the sea-roaming ship, or the shorter journey in the rattling stage or railway car—if, in reading, or musing, or lifting up your heart, you can realize that Saviour's presence, who is about your path and compasses all your ways, you will be almost sorry when such a journey is ended, and when *such* a solitude is exchanged for more wonted society. I can almost believe that John Bunyan left Bedford jail with a sort of trembling, fearing that he might never find again such a Bethel as he had found in that narrow cell for the last twelve years; and I can understand how Samuel Rutherford wrote from his place of banishment,

'Christ hath met me in Aberdeen, and my adversaries have sent me here to be feasted with his love. I would not have believed that there was so much in Jesus as there is. But ' Come and see,' maketh Christ be known in his excellency and glory."

The presence of Christ can turn a dark night into a night much to be remembered. Perhaps it is time to be sleeping, but the November wind is out, and as it riots over the misty hills, and dashes the rain-drift on the rattling casement, and howls like a spirit distracted in the fireless chimney, it has awakened the young sleeper in the upper room. And when his mother enters, she finds him sobbing out his infant fears, or with beating heart hiding from the noisy danger in the depths of his downy pillow. But she puts the candle on the table, and sits down beside the bed; and as he hears her assuring voice, and espies the gay comfort in her smiling face, and as she puts her hand over his, the tear stands still upon his cheek, till it gets time to dry, and the smoothing down of the panic furrows on his brow, and the brightening of his eye announce that he is ready for whatever a mother has got to tell. And as she goes on to explain the mysterious sources of his terror—" That hoarse loud roaring is the brook tumbling over the stones; for the long pouring rains have filled it to the very brim. It is up on the green to-night, and had the cowslips been in blossom they would all have been drowned. Yes—and that thump on the window. It is the old cedar at the corner of the house, and as the wind tosses his stiff branches they bounce and scratch on the panes of glass, and if they were not very small they would be broken in pieces." And then she goes on to tell how this very night there are people out in the pelting blast, whilst her little boy lies warm in his crib, inside of his curtains; and how ships may be upset on the deep sea, or dashed to pieces on rocks so steep that the drowning sailors cannot climb them. And then perhaps she ends it all with breathing a mother's prayer, or he drops asleep beneath the cradle-hymn.

And why describe all this? Because there is so much practical divinity in it. In the history of a child, a night like this is an important night for it has done three things. It has explained some things which, unexplained, would have been a source of constant alarm—perhaps the germ of superstition or insanity. It has taught some precious lessons—sympathy for sufferers, gratitude for mercies, and perhaps some pleasant thought of Him who is the hiding-place from the storm and the covert from the tempest. And then it has deepened in that tender bosom the foundations of filial piety, and helped to give that parent such hold and purchase on a filial heart as few wise mothers have ever failed to win, and no manly son has ever blushed to own.

Then for the parallel. "As one whom his mother comforteth, so the Lord comforteth his people." It is in the dark and boisterous night of sorrow or apprehension that the Saviour reveals himself nigh. And one of the first things he does is to explain the subject matter of the grief, to show its real nature and amount. "It is but a light affliction. It lasts out for a moment. It is a false alarm. It is only the rain-drift on the window—wait till the day dawns and shadows flee away. Wait till morning and you will see the whole extent of it." And then the next thing that he does is to teach some usefu lesson. And during those quiet hours, when the heart is soft, the Saviour's lessons sink deep. And last of all, besides consolation under the trial and peaceful fruits that follow it, by this comforter-visit, the Saviour unspeakably endears himself to that soul. Paul and Silas never knew Christ so well nor loved him so much as after that night which he and they passed together in the Macedonian prison. And the souls on which the Lord Jesus has taken the deepest hold, are those whose great tribulations have thrown them most frequently and most entirely into his own society.

But we hasten to a close. We have seen the meaning of the words so far—Lo, I am with you alway; I am with you to succour in temptation, to strengthen in duty, to guide in perplexity, to comfort in sorrow. From the instant you become a disciple I am with you all along. I am with you every day. All your life I am with you—and at death?—at death you are with me. That's the difference. At present I am always with you, but you are not always with me. At present Jesus is constantly near his own, but his own do not constantly desire to be near him. Here it is only by faith that believers enjoy his presence. There they shall see him as he is. Now the Lord Jesus follows his own whithersoever they go, but they do not always follow him. Then it will be different, for they will follow the Lamb whithersoever he goeth. And all that is wanting to complete the promise is what death's twinkling will supply. Now it is, " Lo, I am with you alway,"—and then it is, " And so shall *we* be ever with the Lord."

" Ever with the Lord." At once and for ever. At once—for absent from the body, we are present with Him. So near is Jesus now, that, like the infant waking from its dream, it looks up, and lo! she sits beside it—waking up from this life-dream, the first sight is Jesus as he is. At once—no flight through immensity—no pilgrimage of the spheres—for the everlasting arms are the first resting-place of the disembodied soul—it will be in the bosom of Immanuel that the emancipated spirit will inquire, " Where am I?" and read in the face of Jesus the answer, " For ever with the Lord." *For ever*—To be with him for a few years, as one way with another John and Peter were—to be with him one Lord's day as the beloved disciple subsequently was—to be with him a few moments, as Paul caught up into the third heavens was—how blessed! But to be ever with the Lord—not only to-day, but to-morrow—nay neither to-day nor to-morrow, but now, now one everlasting now!

> For ever with the Lord!
>   Amen! so let it be;
> Life from the dead is in that word—
>   'Tis immortality

LECTURE III.

THE HEARER OF PRAYER:
THE INTERCESSOR ABOVE:
THE PROMPTER WITHIN.

"Oh thou that hearest prayer."—Psalm lxv. 2.

"Jesus is able to save them to the uttermost that come unto God by him, seeing he ever liveth to make intercession for them.—Heb. vii. 25.

"The Spirit helpeth our infirmities; for we know not what we should pray for as we ought, but the Spirit himself maketh intercession for us with groanings which cannot be uttered."—Rom. viii. 26.

The only proper object of worship is God—the living and true God—Triune Jehovah. Father, Son, and Holy Spirit. According to the nature of the blessings implored or the mercies acknowledged, we have instances of prayer addressed to all the Persons of the blessed Godhead; but the tenor of Scripture shows that in the economy of grace, prayer is usually addressed to the Father through the Son, and by the Holy Ghost. God in Christ is the object of Christian worship, and the author of that worship is the Holy Spirit, as the Spirit of Christ.

I. God is the hearer of prayer.

Dear friends, I am not sure that you all have a distinct conviction of the power of prayer. I am not sure that you all have that confidence in its efficacy, which makes prayer an interesting exercise on ordinary occasions, or a natural and hopeful resource on occasions of perplexity and alarm. As the result of your own musings, or of others' reasonings, you may either have ceased to pray, or you may pray despondingly, as very doubtful if prayer has any power at all, or your so-called prayer may be a series of devout ascriptions without containing a single earnest supplication. I shall read a prayer found among the papers of one of the most amiable of worldly philanthropists as well as one of the most talented of modern jurists. In the single element of gratitude for temporal blessings, it so far surpasses the prayers of many Christians, that we cannot but grieve that it wants what no Christian prayer should want—" The offering of *desires* unto God in the name of Christ."

" Almighty God! Creator of all things! the source of all wisdom, and goodness, and virtue, and happiness, I bow down before thee—not to offer up prayers, for I dare not presume to think or hope that thy most just, unerring, and supreme will can be in any degree influenced by any supplications of mine—nor to pour forth praises and adorations, for I feel that I am unworthy to offer them—but in all humility, and with a deep sense of my own insignificance, to express the thanks of a happy and contented being, for the innumerable benefits which he enjoys. I cannot reflect that I am a human being, living in civilized society, born the member of a free state, the son of virtuous and tender parents, blest with an ample fortune, endowed with faculties which have enabled me to acquire that fortune myself, enjoying a fair reputation, beloved by my relations, esteemed by my friends, thought well of by most of my countrymen to whom my name is known, united to a kind, virtuous, enlightened, and most affectionate wife, the father of seven children, all in perfect health, and all giving by the goodness of their dispositions, a promise of future excellence, and though myself far advanced in life, yet still possessed of health and strength which seem to afford me the prospect of future years of enjoyment. I cannot reflect on all these things and not express my gratitude to thee, O God! from whom all this good has flowed. I am sincerely grateful for all this happiness. I am sincerely grateful for the happiness of all those who are most dear to me, of my beloved wife, of my sweet children, of my relations, and of my friends.

"I prostrate myself, O Almighty and Omniscient God, before thee. In endeavouring to contemplate thy divine attributes, I seek to elevate my soul towards thee; I seek to improve and ennoble my faculties, and to strengthen and quicken my ardour for the public good; and I appear to myself to rise above my earthly existence, while I am indulging the hope that I may at some time prove an humble instrument in the divine work of enlarging the sphere of human happiness."*

This is the thankful but melancholy prayer of a man as virtuous, and, we may add, as devout as any man can be who has not the clear

* "Life of Sir S. Romilly," vol. iii., p 76.

convictions and lively hopes of a believer in Jesus. But even in this act of devotion he does not venture to offer up a single petition,—for he dares not think that the will of the Almighty can in any way be influenced by any supplication of his. And what this gifted lawyer wrote in his meditative retirement, others tacitly think, or openly avow. They feel as if the creation were so vast, and its concerns so multifarious, that it is impossible that even Omniscience can have an ear for all their petitions. Or they feel that the Creator is so exalted,—his throne so high and lifted up,—that it is not fit for them to approach it. Or they feel that the laws of nature are so fixed, and the decrees of the Eternal so determinate, that it is only presumption to expect that any earnestness or importunity of theirs can alter them. Such thoughts do arise in some men's hearts. By some they are sported flippantly, by others they are felt painfully; but they are as erroneous as they are fatal to hope and effort, as preposterous as they are paralyzing; and a few considerations, carefully pondered, may, by the blessing of God, set your minds conclusively at rest on this and like misgivings.

And first of all, it must be remembered, that the human mind has a much greater talent at asking questions than at answering them, and many minds have a greater propensity to raise doubts and start difficulties, than to repose in that scanty measure of truth which is already ascertained and infallible. I am speaking not of things *necessary*, but of things *contingent*; and by truth ascertained and infallible, I mean knowledge which does not rest on mere *opinion*, but knowledge which comes to us in the shape of *information*. Anything which I am told by a credible witness is information, and so is any thing which comes to my knowledge through any of my own five senses, and so is any knowledge that I gain directly by attending to the processes and feelings of my own mind. But any notion which does not come from one or other of these three legitimate sources,—sensation, consciousness, or competent testimony,—is good for nothing. It may be an ingenious hypothesis, or a plausible opinion, but it is not matter of fact; it is not information. Till it assume a positive form it is not knowledge, and I have no security for its eventual truth.

Now, excepting mathematical truth, which has no connexion with the present subject, we repeat, that the human mind can attain no sure and infallible knowledge, except that which it gets in the positive form; that knowledge for which it has the evidence of its own senses or personal consciousness, or the senses and consciousness of others. Beyond this the human mind cannot go. If they be not the limited facts which we have discovered for ourselves, for all beyond we are at the mercy of others who know better than ourselves—that is, of others who have seen and felt and handled what we have not— and to expect to come at absolute knowledge in any other way is to expect an impossibility.— The hawk may fly higher than the sparrow, and the eagle, again, may soar above them both, but none of them can rise beyond the atmosphere.

LECTURE III.

An European may know more than a savage, and a scholar may know more than either; but none of them can know for certain anything except *facts*, which they have observed for themselves, or facts which have been revealed to them by others.

But whilst these are the limits of human certainty, they are not the limits of human curiosity. In our anxiety to be wise, beyond what is ascertainable, we have invented a transcendental Metaphysics,—a science on which the acutest of human intellects have bestowed themselves, and to whose literature some of the most eloquent argument and finest fancy of ancient times and modern has been contributed—but a science which, amidst all its curious questions and doubtsome answers—the accumulation of two thousand years—has not added a single atom to the domain of ascertained truth or actual knowledge. If you could conceive the fowls of heaven suddenly seized with a strong desire to get away from this globe altogether,—if you could imagine them all at different elevations in the atmosphere, according to the strength of their pinions, or the lightness of their forms, but all, beak uppermost, struggling and fluttering, and screwing their way a little and a little higher in the rarified medium you would have a very exact idea of the object of metaphysical inquiry, and the position of its several votaries. Its object is to ascertain truths regarding which we have no information, and there may doubtless be many such truths,—but are they ascertainable? There are other planets besides this one, and we have supposed the case of the fowls of heaven wishing to reach them,—but are they accessible? A bird of powerful pinion, or singular lightness, may rise a mile above his fluttering competitors, and as an affair of aerial gymnastics, the fruitless effort may be good practice; but the wing which is farthest above the surface is still a thousand times farther from the next nearest world; and so in the metaphysical contest to get away from the regions of absolute information—the *terra firma* of positive truth, there has been a wonderful display of mental power and buoyancy, but the subtile spirit which has mounted the highest above the ascertained and the actual of our restricted humanity, is still infinitely distant from the next nearest domain of knowledge. As some one has truly remarked, "To know more, we first must be more."*

It is not a popular doctrine, but it is one to which the world is slowly coming round—of contingent truth we can know nothing regarding which we have not positive information, and beyond these limits to wonder what things there are, or how such and such things can be, is to vex ourselves in vain. Those things which I have observed for myself, and those which others have told me, make up a solid basis of truth,—a *terra firma* of fact. If I am dissatisfied with its narrow limits, I may fling myself over into the abyss of speculation, and finding in every deep a deeper still, perish at last in total scepticism; or I may try to soar upwards into a transcendental region, and after fruitless efforts to be wise be-

* Lewes' "History of Philosophy."

yond my nature's capacity, be content to fold my weary pinions at last on the homely landing-place of common sense and tangible truth. There, and there only, on the solid ground of information, on the firm footing of what I have observed for myself, or others have told me, can I find a permanent rest for my spirit, and a secure starting-point for eternity.

Applying these principles to the case before us, we do not ask what anterior probabilities are there that prayer is heard and answered? But what proof? Can we say from our own experience, or have we reason to believe, on competent authority, that prayer has actual power?

Now, it is conclusive on the entire subject, that for the efficacy of prayer we have the assurance of God himself. "The eyes of the Lord are over the righteous, and his ears are open unto their prayers." "Delight thyself in the Lord, and he shall give thee the desires of thine heart." "Commit thy way unto the Lord; trust also in him, and he shall bring it to pass." "Call upon me in the day of trouble, and I will answer thee." And lest we should desire more definite information we have it. "No man hath seen God at any time,—the only-begotten Son, who is in the bosom of the Father, he hath declared him." There was once amongst us one who knew precisely the reception which prayers are wont to meet with in the Court of Heaven. There was once on earth one who could testify, on this matter, what he had seen, and who could tell distinctly whether the prayers of earth are audible in the upper sanctuary, and how far the high and

Holy One is disposed to regard and answer them; and nothing can be more encouraging than the language of this Faithful Witness. "When thou prayest, enter into thy closet; and when thou hast shut thy door, pray to thy Father who is in secret; and thy Father who seeth in secret shall reward thee openly." "I say unto you, that if two of you shall agree on earth, as touching anything that they shall ask, it shall be done for them of my Father who is in heaven." "Whatsoever ye shall ask in my name, that will I do, that the Father may be glorified in the Son." "Ask, and it shall be given you; seek, and ye shall find; knock, and it shall be opened unto you: for every one that asketh receiveth; and he that seeketh findeth; and to him that knocketh it shall be opened."

So conclusive are these and similar declarations, that no farther warrant should be needful to give precision and hopeful earnestness to our petitions. We have the living God himself assuring us that he is prepared to accept, and consider, and answer them; and we have the Son of God himself come down from the bosom of the Father, the appointed medium of communication betwixt heaven and earth; we have the Intercessor himself declaring, that no petition passes through his hand but it brings back its blessing; and farther assurances than these should scarcely be needful to make the man who is conscious of sincerity in prayer secure of an answer. But farther assurance is given. It should be enough that we have historic evidence that the Lord has promised to answer prayer; but, over and above, we have historic evidence that, times almost unnumbered, he *has* answered it. In the lives of Abraham and Abraham's servant, of Lot, of Jacob, of Moses, Joshua, Gideon, Manoah and Samson, of Hannah and of Samuel, of David the king and Solomon his son, Hezekiah and Manasseh, of the prophets Elijah, Elisha, Jeremiah, Daniel, and Ezekiel; then, again, in the history of the apostles and the early Church,* we have abundant evidence that, whatever may have become of our own, others have directed prevailing supplications to the Heavenly Majesty, and that singular mercies have been, from time to time, bestowed in answer to believing prayer.

And here you would not wonder though we should close the case. Having God's promise and the Saviour's assurance of the prevalency of prayer, and having, both in the sacred narrative and later histories, so many cases recorded of accepted and answered supplications, there is enough to justify the conclusion, that men ought always to pray, and not to faint. But there is an evidence, to most minds more satisfactory than the most harmonious testimony—I mean, the evidence of personal consciousness—the proof they have from their own experience. There have been persons who possessed this proof; and I believe almost every Christian could make, at some stage of his progress the same entry in his journal as John Newton,† when he wrote:—

* See Fincher's "Achievements of Prayer,"—a delightful work containing in the words of Scripture the different prayers with their answers as recorded there

† Quoted in M'Gill on "Closet Prayer."

"About this time I began to know that there is a God who hears and answers prayer." We believe that, to most real Christians here present, the whole discussion of this morning will be superfluous, and, so far as they are personally concerned, uninteresting; for their short argument in favour of the practice, and conclusive answer to all objections, is the Psalmist's own:—"But verily God hath heard me; he hath attended to the voice of my prayer." The efficacy of prayer is with them no longer a matter of probability or a subject for reasoning. It is now a matter of fact—an ascertained and positive truth—a truth not even of others' testimony, but a fact of their own consciousness. And so, brethren, if you wish to have your minds set conclusively at rest on the subject, like the Psalmist, pray—pray till, like the Psalmist, you can sing—"I love the Lord, because he hath heard my voice and my supplications. Because he hath inclined his ear unto me, therefore will I call upon him as long as I live."

And now, having put on its proper footing, as a matter of fact, the truth that God is the hearer of prayer, the speculative difficulties with which some have perplexed the subject need give us no pain. If the truth be *ascertained*, and the mind of the man who has discovered it be sound and vigorous, no difficulties will disturb his faith. To use the words of a clear thinker,*—" Before a confessed and unconquerable difficulty, the mind, if in a healthy state, reposes as quietly as

* Arnold's " Sermons Interpretation of Scripture."
p. 147.

when in possession of a discovered truth—as quietly and contentedly as we are accustomed to bear that law of our nature which denies us the power of seeing through all space, or of being exempt from sickness and decay." Allow that some serious objections could be started against the efficacy of prayer, these objections do not touch the evidence on which we believe that God has promised to hear prayer, nor that other evidence on which we believe that he has actually heard and answered it. The greatness of creation and the littleness of man, the decrees of God and the immutability of natural laws, would not stop his prayer, nor startle from his knees the man who could say—" Verily, God hath heard me: he hath attended to the voice of my petition;" but, superior to all speculative difficulties, because secure in his experimental knowledge, that wise and happy man would still pray on. And, to see the wisdom of this course, you have only to put a parallel case. In the infinite variety of this universe, there may be a world where the processes of growth, and decay, and reproduction, so familiar to us, are utterly unknown. Suppose that the inhabitant of such a world were transported to our own, and that he witnessed the husbandman's operations in spring. He might marvel what he meant. He might wonder why he cast these grains of corn into the ground; and, when told that it was with a view to reproduce them a hundred-fold, the mysterious process might at once assume the aspect of infatuation, and he might begin to remonstrate with the labourer on this crazy waste of useful corn; and, if this visitor from Jupiter or Saturn were as acute a metaphysician as many in our own world are, he might adduce many subtile arguments—too subtile, perhaps, for a farmer to refute. " Is not this a mad notion of yours? Do you really mean to affirm, that this particle of corn will grow into a hundred more? Nay, do you pretend to say that you will put into that hole this hard and husky atom, and come back in three months and find it changed into the glossy stems, the waving leaves, and rustling ears, of the tall wheat-stalk? What resemblance, or what adequacy, is there between that seed and a sheaf of corn? Besides, if a buried grain is to grow up a hundred-fold, why don't you bury diamonds and guineas, and get them multiplied after the same proportion? Besides, O simpleton! do you not know that all these matters have been fixed and settled from everlasting? It has been fore-ordained, either that you are to have a crop next autumn, or that you are to have none. In the former case, your present pains are needless, for you will get your harvest without all this ado. If the latter, your pains are useless, for nothing will procure you a crop where it is not the purpose of Omnipotence that you should have one." Did the ploughman listen to all this remonstrance, he might be much perplexed with it. He might not be able to show the precise way in which seeds exert an efficacy on the future crop; and he might not see at once the reason why corn-grains should be reproductive, whilst diamonds and guineas are not; and, least of all, might he be able to dispose of the fatalist objection. But he would deem it enough to refute all this mystification to say—that he had never known a harvest without a seed-time and that he had never sown sufficiently without reaping something. And so, when a man comes in from the prayerless world, and starts his objections, a praying man may not be able to discuss them one by one—he may not even understand them—" But this I know, God is the hearer of prayer, and, verily, he hath heard myself." And, like the farmer, who scatters his seed heedless of all that has ever been said on necessity, and causation, and general laws, a wise believer will, in the face of hypothetic difficulties, proceed on ascertained facts, and, amidst objections and cavils, will persist to pray, and continue to enjoy the blessings which prayer procures.

Though hitherto I have not touched these theoretic difficulties, I may now, in conclusion, mention three simple truths, in whose successive light every doubt and difficulty should melt away. God is the hearer of prayer,—

1. Because he is the Living God.
2. Because he is Almighty.
3. And because he is the God of Love.

1. Jehovah is the Living God. " The tendency of many minds is to regard the Deity as a principle rather than as a person."* They look upon him as a power—a presence—a principle— the most general of general laws—not as the great I Am, the Living God. No wonder that they have little heart to pray. If Elijah had known no other deity than the little cloud, or the sea from which it ascended, or the sky in which

* Chalmers' " Natural Theology," vol. ii., p 315.

it floated, or the electric action which condensed more and more dark vapour round it, he would scarcely have renewed his supplication seven times. But he addressed himself not to clouds, but to the Living God of Israel. When I go to my friend's house to procure some favour from him, I do not speak to his books or his furniture —I do not invoke his genius or guardian spirit; I do not apostrophise the abstract idea of benevolence, or virtue, or friendship; but I speak direct to himself, a lowly friend, it may be, or an unworthy suppliant—but still a living man, I address a living person. Prayer is not an appeal to dead matter or to general laws. It is not a request to the rain to fall, or to the sun to stand still. It is not imploring the principle of gravitation to relax its rule on my behalf and disengage my feet from the earth, or beseeching the fire to forbear and not burn me. It is not to supplicate such virtues as meekness and patience and fortitude to come down and take up their abode in my bosom. But when I pray I address myself to that Living God who has the elements of nature at his control, and, what is to me, as an immortal and accountable being, far more important, who has at his disposal infinite resources for making his creatures holy. He is the *Living* God; and if, in asking mercies from him, I may not be as sanguine as a friend when he entreats a friend or a child when he importunes a father, I may at least be as earnest and urgent as a subject is when he has opportunity to ply his suit with his living sovereign.

2. But some who restrain prayer do err from

not knowing the power of God. They feel as if it were impossible even for Omniscience to attend to every suppliant, and beyond the power even of Omnipotence to bestow a separate boon in answer to each petition. Or they feel as if they were only the more important requests of the more eminent suitors that are likely to be noticed and conceded. But what is Omnipotence? Is it not the power of attending to all things undistracted, as well as of doing the mightiest things unexhausted? The Almighty—is he not able to attend to all the wants of all his creatures? Is there in creation aught that would lead us to suppose that to his comprehensive eye any grandeur is imposing, or any minuteness despicable? Did he only create the suns and larger planets, and leave it to moons and little worlds to create themselves? Or, coming down to this lower world, did he bestow a higher finish on the bulkier existences, and show little care for the lesser and lower? Was he rejoicing in the greatness of his strength when he formed the oak and the lion, and had his arm grown weary when it reached the lily and the nightingale? Though there were no Bible to proclaim it, there is evidence enough—whether we look up into the heavens with their circling worlds, or down into a drop of water with its myriad of gay darting monads—proof enough that He who *made* the whole of such a universe is able to *attend* to it all. There is proof enough that no multitude of suppliants can distract him and no magnitude of their requests exhaust Him. There is proof enough that if any prayer be unanswered, it is not because the offerer was too little, nor because he asked too much.

3. And others err, forgetting God's goodness. True, Jehovah may be the Living God, and a God of boundless power; but what if he be a hard master or an angry king? What if we ourselves have put him in an attitude of estrangement, and the same breath which addresses him in the language of entreaty, what if it has previously assailed the High and Holy One in tones of hostility? Here does come in a difficulty on which conjecture could only throw a more perplexing light. The hearer of prayer, is he not also the hater of sin? And coming into his presence, instead of procuring blessings, may I not be provoking a more swift displeasure? Here is indeed a difficulty—the gloomier alternative of which our own guilty consciences too severely favour, and from which we should have found no sure escape, had not the heavenly High Priest, reposing in the Father's love, and holding out to his guilty brethren his hand of mediation, said, " After this manner pray ye, ' *Our Father*, which art in heaven.' "

Nothing shows so strikingly that God is willing to hear and answer prayer as the provision he has made for its acceptable and effectual presentation. However worthless the suppliant, he may present his petition in the name of God's beloved Son; and however dim his ideas and powerless his expressions, he may obtain as the instigator of his desires and the guide of his devotion, none other than the Spirit of God.

11. Where prayer is offered in Jesus' name, he maketh intercession with the Father.

Jesus sits on the Father's right hand, and there he intercedes for his people. This is just the sequel and continuation of Redemption. Just as God's Providence is the preserving of his creation once he has formed it, so Christ's intercession is the preserving of his Church now that he has bought it. The Mediator's presence within the veil secures the perseverance of his people till they too be within it. For Christ maketh intercession for us. He sees some Peter at this moment about to be sifted as wheat, and he prays that his faith fail not. He sees a child of light walking in darkness, or some forlorn disciple like to faint by the way, and he prays the Father, and he sends the Comforter. He sees a band of sore-tempted disciples. He espies a Lot in Sodom, or a Daniel in the den—a Joseph in Egypt, or a saint in Sardis, and he says, " Holy Father, keep through thine own name those whom thou hast given me. Keep them from the evil." He sees a believer waxing formal and cold, restraining prayer and disrelishing the word; and he says, " Sanctify them through thy truth ; and then the sickness comes which drives him back to the throne of grace, or the sorrow which sends him to the word again; and finding out a multitude of undetected sins and lacking graces, the believer is sanctified anew. And oh! he rises eagerly from his royal seat; for yonder is a believer dying; he " stands "* up at the right hand of God, for a Stephen is about to fall on sleep, and the Inter-

* Acts vii. 56.

cessor cries, "Father, I will that they also whom thou hast given me, be with me where I am, that they may behold my glory." The Father wills, and the Lord Jesus receives that spirit.

But although, so to speak, on the part of God, "all things are ready;" though he sits on his throne of grace, and though the Mediator waits with his golden censer to receive and then to offer up the prayers of sinners here on earth—all things are not ready on the part of the sinner. Diffidence Godward, dimness of perception, coldness of desire, perversity of will, and distraction of spirit, are all so many "infirmities" under which each petitioner labours; and it is for the "help of these "infirmities" that the God of grace has provided not only an Advocate above but a prompter within.

III. The Holy Spirit guides the thoughts and instigates the desires—he helps the infirmities of believers when they pray.

1. Guilt on the conscience is one great hinderance to prayer. When sin is recent—when, like Adam skulking among the trees, the bittersweet of the forbidden fruit is still present to his taste, and his newly-opened eyes are aghast at his own deformity—it is not natural for the self-condemned transgressor to draw near to God. And it is not till the Spirit of God directs his view to the unnoticed sacrifice, and encourages him to put on the robe of God's providing, that the abashed and trembling criminal can venture back into God's presence. And it is not till the Spirit of God comes forth into his soul, and begins to cry "Abba" there, that the soul goes

forth with alacrity to meet a reconciled God To reveal the great High Priest, the daysman betwixt Infinite Holiness and human vileness—to open heaven and display Jesus standing at the right hand of God—to impart confidence in the finished work, and so, amidst abounding guilt, to give hope to prayer—is His work who, when he is come, convinces not only of sin, but of righteousness.*

2. Another great hinderance to prayer is dimness of spiritual perception. When a man of taste or science climbs a mountain in a bright, transparent day, he rejoices in its goodly prospect or curious spoils; but his dog feels no interest in them. He sees the philosopher peering through his telescope, or exploring for the little plants that grow near the summit, or splintering the rocks and putting fragments in the bag; but it never occurs to the spaniel so much as to marvel what his master is finding there. He sits yawning and panting on a sunny knoll, or snaps at the mountain-bee as it comes sailing past him, or chases the conies back into their holes, and scampers down, with noisy glee, as soon as the sad durance is over. The disparity between the philosopher and his irrational friend is hardly greater than it is between the believer and the worldling when you bring them together into the domain of faith. " The natural man perceiveth not the things of the Spirit of God," and on the Pisgah of the same revelation whence the believer descries a goodly land, and where he is making the most interesting discoveries, the other

* John xvi 8.

sees nothing to arrest his attention. The word of God and its promises—the throne of grace and its privileges—the things of faith in all their varieties—have no existence to worldly men. And when constrained to bear others company in outward ordinances, they are thankful when the ended prayer or the closing sanctuary sends them back to the world again. But just as the same lover of nature might ascend his favourite eminence on a future day, and find all his goodly prospects intercepted by a baffling mist, so dense that, except a pebble here and there, he can alight on none of its rare productions, and without any opening vista by which he can catch a glimpse of the fair regions around: so the believer may ascend the hill of God—he may open his Bible or enter his closet—and find, alas! that it is a foggy day, the beauteous panorama blotted out and himself left to grope chillily in the cold and perplexing gloom. But, like a gale of summer wind upspringing and lifting all the fog from the mountain-top, the breath of the Omnipotent Spirit can scatter every cloud and leave the soul on a pinnacle of widest survey, rejoicing in the purest light of God.

3. A third infirmity of the saints, and a great hinderance to prayer, is the feebleness of affection Godward. Human affection is an intermitting spring. Even though the covert streams which feed it should be always flowing, it is only now and then, when the fountain is filled up to the brim, that there is a momentary overflow. There may be a very deep attachment between the members of a family; and yet it is only on some

casual occasion—the day of their re-union after long separation, or the eve of parting, or one of those propitious seasons when people realize how happy is their lot—that the fountain overflows and they give utterance to their irrepressible emotions. But owing to this deficiency of ardour—this infrequency of their fits of fervent affection—it comes to pass that the members of a harmonious family will be much together, and yet not take full advantage of their opportunities of mutual intercourse, nor grow remarkably in mutual acquaintance or mutual endearment. This infirmity of human affection extends into the realm of faith. There is a real affection on the part of the believer toward his Father in heaven; but it is often latent—often languid—not always welling up and flowing over—and it often requires some special incident of mercy or of judgment to swell it up to that point which makes himself conscious of its presence. Just as separations, threatened or actual, bring out the love of friends to one another, so a decree, like that of Darius interdicting prayer, or a flight, like that of David from the house of God to the land of Jordan. brings out the believer's love to his Heavenly Father—reveals it to himself. And just as sudden acts of kindness surprise former friends into a fonder and more outspoken affection, so the unlooked-for arrival of some astounding mercy will startle the believer into such thankfulness or self-abasement as will transport him instantly to the throne of grace. But, even apart from any present visitation of judgment or mercy, there are influences which will, from time to time, surcharge the believing soul with gratitude, or adoration, or earnestness after God ; and, just as in life's daily tenor there are auspicious moments when memory or an open eye discloses, in all the zest of novelty, the excellence of a familiar friend, so there are genial hours in the believer's history when the Spirit, the Enlightener and Remembrancer, brings to view such attractions in that all-sufficient Friend whom we so readily forget, that the enraptured soul looks on and wonders, and desires no greater blessedness. Reverting to our original emblem : as the intermitting fountain takes a long interval to fill it in a dry and sultry season, but fills the faster and overflows the oftener as the mountain is bathed in abundant dews, and may at last, amidst the plenteous rain, become a constant stream ; so, as the believer's heart is filled with more rapid love and joy by the Spirit's plentiful downpouring, the rare and intermitting spring of supplication flows more frequently, till, anon, it becomes—not a daily—but a constant emanation, and that full-souled and heaven-replenished saint has learned to " pray without ceasing."

4. Another infirmity of the saints is a disposition to ask wrong things. We know not what to pray for as we ought. The blessings for which it is most natural to pray, are those which we least need—temporal mercies. There are often an urgency and importunity for these strangely disproportionate to the earnestness with which we beg the better gifts. Sometimes the believer prays the Lord that the thorn in the flesh may depart from him, far more eagerly than he

asks that sufficient grace which will make the thorn no longer painful, or even will enable him to glory in infirmity. Again, amongst spiritual mercies, believers do not always covet most earnestly the best gifts, or the gifts which in their circumstances would be best for them. It was good for Peter and James and John to be on the holy mount, and they prayed to tarry there. But it was good for the world, and eventually good for themselves, that they were obliged to come down. It is natural for believers to covet rapture and elevation more intensely than hard labour and hazardous testimonies for Jesus, and a toilsome pilgrimage through a hostile world—but for both themselves and that world, it is better that they should go down to active service—remembering, however, what they heard and saw when they were with Jesus on the mount.

But the Holy Spirit knows the actual state of each. He knows what spiritual blessings the suppliant really needs, and what temporal mercies it would be no eventual blessing for him to attain. If it be a dangerous temporal good, he can wean the soul from the vehement desire of it; or by exhibiting some surpassing heavenly good can awaken such longings after *that* as will make the other be forgotten; or by simply reconciling the soul to the adorable will of God, can make it content to merge its own instinctive longings in his majestic sovereignty. Then again he can so reveal to the soul its actual necessities, that praying time will not be expended in imploring undesired mercies, or confessing unfelt deficiency. He knows the things which accord with the will of God, and teaches the petitioner to ask those blessings in asking which he can plead God's precept or God's promise.

5. A fifth infirmity of the saints is that, even when asking right things, they do not ask in a manner agreeable to the will of God. Some are haunted by worldly and frivolous thoughts in prayer, and feel as if their minds were never so silly and trifling, so cloddish and carnal, as when they attempt to pray. It would seem as if all the vanities of the week came crowding into their minds—as if on signal given—the moment they went upon their knees—and petitions for the most stupendous blessings will be ascending, without force or meaning, through a swarm of idle fancies and vagrant thoughts. Or perhaps, amidst greater composure of spirit, there may be little or no longing after the blessing asked. The suppliant begs it, not so much because he appreciates or desires it, as because he thinks it dutiful to make mention of it, and after a formal enumeration of unsought mercies, he goes his way without having actually lodged one prevailing request—one effectual fervent prayer before the throne of grace. Or perhaps amidst considerable earnestness and urgency, the believer is embarrassed and distressed by the unsuitableness of his thoughts—his mean conceptions of those unspeakable benefits for which he is entreating, and his unworthy thoughts of that God with whom he has to do. Now, for all these distractions in sacred duties, the remedy lies with the Spirit himself. We can shut to the door; but he can shut the heart, and lock out the world and all its

phantoms We can open the Bible and look at the promises; but he can open heaven and show each promise in its glorious fulfilment. We can lift our eyes towards the hills; but he can show us " Him who is invisible," and can enable our souls to rest on him with the sweetest security for the fulfilment of all that he has spoken We can task ourselves to stated times of devotion and resolve that we shall spend a given space in prayer; but he can so enlarge the heart—he can make the spirit so strong in the Lord and in the power of his might—he can fill the mind with such longings after angelic purity—such delight in heavenly things—such vehement aspirations after God; he can intercede within us with those yearnings and groanings which cannot be uttered, so that hours and minutes shall not be counted, and the untiring soul continues "instant in prayer."

LECTURE IV.

THE PRIVILEGE OF PRAYER.

"Rejoice evermore. Pray without ceasing."
1 Thess. v. 16, 17.

"The Athenians spent their time in nothing else, but either to tell or to hear some new thing;" and whatever may have become of the Attic elegance and the Attic genius, modern society is not deficient in the Athenian curiosity. Nor do we blame it. The desire of novelty is not in itself blameworthy; but there is one form of it which we would like to see more frequent. To *freshen* old truths is nearly as important as to discover new ones; and instead of telling or hearing some new thing, our time would often be as advantageously occupied in thinking over, and brightening up the meaning of some *old* thing.

Few expressions in theology are older than that which speaks of the "privilege of prayer:" but nothing could be a greater novelty in the history of some who now hear me, than to find prayer an actual privilege. Am I wrong? "The privilege of prayer!" Do not some feel that the *burden* of prayer,—the *obligation*, the *duty*, would be a truer name for it? Do not some of you feel, that to call it a *privilege* is just to give a pleasant name to an irksome thing? If so, instead of initiating you in a new science, that individual would do you a better service who should give you fresh light on this old truth, and make you feel, that not only has prayer power with God, but it is very nearly the highest privilege of man.

Let us make a supposition.* Suppose that the individual in this kingdom, who combines in himself, the greatest wisdom and goodness, were accessible to you. Suppose that when anything pressed upon you,—a difficulty from which your own sagacity could not extricate you, or an undertaking which your own resources could not compass,—you had only to send him a statement of the case, and were sure, in good time, to get his best and kindest counsel,—would not you deem this a great *privilege?* Would not something of this sort just meet the case of many here? One is entering on a new course of occupation, and in its very outset meets with problems that fairly baffle him, but which a friend of a little more experience or perspicacity could instantly solve. Another is overtaken by a sea of troubles,—a concourse of trials which quite overwhelm him, but through which he perfectly believes that a stronger arm or a more buoyant spirit could carry him. But where shall he look for that wiser friend,—that stronger arm? Suppose, again, that when in sudden danger or in deep distress, there were some way by which

---

* This was suggested by a similar idea in a Lecture of John Foster, as preserved in the MS notes of an intelligent hearer.

you could make known your situation, to a spirit departed. That spirit is now far wiser than he was when on earth. He has sources of knowledge that are not open to you, and he has powers not yet possessed by you. Suppose that in grief or in difficulty you could invoke him. Suppose that there were some process by which you could arrest his ear among the glorified, and in the lapse of a brief moment bring him though unseen to your side; and suppose that, to this spirit made perfect, the spirit of your departed parent, or of some one remarkable for his wisdom and sanctity, you could detail the whole matter that grieves and perplexes you, and though there should be no response from the viewless shade, you knew that he had heard you, and was away to interpose effectively on your behalf,—would you not feel much comforted and lightened? Would you not resume your own active exertions with far greater hopefulness,—assured that there would now attend them a power beyond what was proper to them, or inherent in yourself? But farther, suppose that instead of any wise or influential personage on earth, or any glorified spirit in paradise, it was possible for you to secure the ear and engage the help of one of the principalities or powers in the heavenly places; some being of such bright intelligence, that he can smile at all our wisdom, and such commanding might, that he can do in a moment what would occupy our race for a millennium; could you for an instant bespeak his attention, and gain assurance of his willingness to help; would you not feel that your object was unspeakably promoted, or your burden amazingly lightened? To have enlisted such ability and skill upon your side,—the few minutes spent in securing such superhuman help,—would you not feel that they were a larger contribution towards eventual success than a life-time of your personal efforts? But rise a step higher—an infinite step!—and suppose that it were possible to arrest the ear and secure the help of God himself; suppose that you could, by any possibility, gain the attention of the living God,—that you could secure not the cold and distant on-looking, but the interested regard and the omnipotent interposition of Jehovah himself,—would not this be a privilege? But this is precisely what prayer is. Some have no friend of extraordinary sagacity or power to go to. The spirits of the departed cannot come to us; and neither to them nor to angels are we warranted to pray. And even though we could evoke a Samuel from the sepulchre, or bring down Gabriel from above the sky,—the blessings which are most needful for us are such as neither Samuel nor Gabriel can give,—blessings of which the treasure lies within the light inaccessible, and of which Omnipotence alone preserves the key. That Almighty hand prayer moves. That incommunicable key prayer turns. That unapproachable treasury prayer opens. The blessings which Solomon in all his glory, and Abraham in the bosom of his God, and the seraphs who overshadow the throne,—the blessings which these have not to give, it is the privilege of prayer to procure.

But set it in another light. Imagine that there

had been certain limitations on prayer. Imagine that there had only been one spot on the earth from which prayer could arise with acceptance. Imagine—by no means inconceivable, for there was once something very like it—imagine that the Lord had selected some little spot of earth— a Mount Zion or a Holy Land—and said that here, and here only, was the place to worship. Imagine that from this hallowed spot alone there had existed a passage into heaven for the prayers of earth, and that all supplications, however earnest, uttered on the profane soil of the common globe, had gone for nothing. What a resorting we should have seen to this place of only prevalency! When there occurred some conjuncture decisive of weal or woe to an individual or a family, or when a man became so anxious about his soul's salvation that nothing could content him save light from above, we should have seen the busy trader arranging for his protracted absence, and the cautious, untravelled husbandman preparing for the perilous pilgrimage, and multitudes, on their own behalf or on behalf of others, resorting to the place where prayer is heard and answered. And imagine, farther, that there had just been one day in the year when prayer was permitted; that those who arrived at the appointed place too late, found the gate of access closed for the next twelve months, and, however sudden the emergency, and however extreme its exigency, that it was impossible to do anything for it till the weary year moved round, and brought back the one propitious day!—even thus restricted, would not prayer have been felt to be a privilege worth a pilgrimage and worth a long on-waiting? Just fancy that in our earth's yearly revolution round the sun there was disclosed a crevice in the sky! —that on one night in the year, and on one mountain top, there was a vista opened through the encircling vault, and a sight of dazzling glories revealed to all who gazed from the favoured summit;—and fancy that through the brilliant gap there fell a shower of gold and gems, and that this recurred regularly on the self-same evening every year, what a concourse to that Pisgah might you count upon! How many eager eyes would strain the breathless hour beforehand till the first streak of radiance betokened the bursting glory! And how many emulous hands would rush together to catch the flaming rubies and the diamond-rain!

And just conceive—the only other supposition we shall make—that certain costly or arduous preliminaries were essential in order to successful prayer; suppose that a day's strict abstinence, or some painful self-punishment, were exacted; or that each worshipper were required to bring in his hand some costly offering—the choicest of his flock, or a large per centage on his income— And who would say that this was unreasonable? Would not access into God's own presence—a favour so ineffable—would it not be wisely purchased at any price, and might not sinful "dust and ashes" marvel that after any ordeal or purifying process it was admitted near such Majesty?

But how stands the case? Prayer is not a consultation with the highest wisdom which this world can supply. It is not intercourse with an angel or a spirit made perfect. But it is an approach to the living God. It is access to the High and Holy One who inhabiteth eternity. It is detailing in the ear of Divine sympathy every sorrow. It is consulting with Divine wisdom on every difficulty. It is asking from Divine resources the supply of every want. And this not once in a life-time, or for a few moments on a stated day of each year, but at any moment, at every time of need. Whatever be the day of your distress, it is a day when prayer is allowable. Whatever be the time of your calamity, it is a time when prayer is available. However early in the morning you seek the gate of access, you find it already open; and however deep the midnight moment when you find yourself in the sudden arms of death, the winged prayer can bring an instant Saviour near. And this wheresoever you are. It needs not that you ascend some special Pisgah or Moriah. It needs not that you should enter some awful shrine, or put off your shoes on some holy ground. Could a memento be reared on every spot from which an acceptable prayer has passed away, and on which a prompt answer has come down, we should find *Jehovah-shammah*—" the Lord hath been here"— inscribed on many a cottage hearth and many a dungeon floor. We should find it not only in Jerusalem's proud temple and David's cedar galleries, but in the fisherman's cottage by the brink of Gennesaret, and in the upper chamber where Pentecost began. And whether it be the field where Isaac went to meditate, or the rocky knoll where Jacob lay down to sleep, or the brook where Israel wrestled, or the den where Daniel gazed on the hungry lions and the lions gazed on him, or the hill-sides where the Man of Sorrows prayed all night, we should still discern the prints of the ladder's feet let down from heaven—the landing-place of mercies because the starting-point of prayers. And all this whatsoever you are. It needs no saint, no proficient in piety, no adept in eloquent language, no dignity of earthly rank. It needs but a simple Hannah, or a lisping Samuel. It needs but a blind beggar, or a loathsome lazar. It needs but a penitent publican, or a dying thief. And it needs no sharp ordeal, no costly passport, no painful expiation to bring you to the mercy-seat; or rather, I should say, it needs the costliest of all; but the blood of atonement—the Saviour's merit—the name of Jesus—priceless as they are, cost the sinner nothing. They are freely put at his disposal, and instantly and constantly he may use them. This access to God in every place, at every moment, without any price or any personal merit, is it not a privilege?

And yet this old truth, I am anxious, before we part, that you should find in it new significance; and therefore, to make it somewhat more specific, let me apply it to a few cases, probably all represented here.

1. "Is any among you afflicted? Let him pray." "In agony nature is no atheist. The mind which knows not where to fly, flies to God."* And to spring into the arms of Omni-

Hannah More on Prayer, p. 153.

potence, to find refuge in the bosom of Mercy, is to weep no longer. The drowning man whose last sensation was the weltering brine; who felt the seething flood go over him, and as he settled down among the trailing weeds, the memory of home darted like a death-shot through his heart and put an end to other anguish;—when that rescued man opens his eyes beneath some friendly roof, and instead of the watery winding-sheet and the crawling gulf-monsters, finds himself on a couch of warm comfort, his chamber glowing with the cheerful faggot, a friendly face ready to greet his first waking, and see through the window the ship that is waiting to bear him back to his native isle,—it may be true that he had treasures in the foundered vessel, and that some curious or precious things he was carrying home may never be fished up from the devouring deep,—but how different his lot from the poor castaway, whom the billows have landed on a desolate rock, and who creeping about in his dripping rags, can find no food but the limpets, no fuel but the crackling sea-weed, no hovel to shelter him, and no sail to waft him away. Both have been wrecked, and both have lost their all; but in the joy of his rescue the one forgets his poverty, and in his wretched asylum from the waves the other recognizes nothing but a prison and a tomb. Precisely similar is the case of the afflicted man who prays, and of him who, when afflicted, cannot pray—the man whom the billows land on the desolate rock of worldliness or atheism, and the man who, from the stun of drowning waters, wakes up in the pavilion of God's own presence. Both may have suffered equal losses. Both may have left a treasure in the deep. Both may have been washed empty handed ashore. But the man of prayer is like the man who comes to himself in the asylum of the friendly home. The bliss of present fellowship with God abates or banishes the grief of recent loss. On the lee-shore, which has shattered his frail bark, he is astonished to lift up his eyes and find himself the inmate of a beloved friend, and a familiar dwelling. He knows that he will land safe at last, and is happy even now. "Is any among you afflicted? Let him pray."

2. Is any among you perplexed? "If any of you lack wisdom, let him ask of God, who giveth to all men liberally, and upbraideth not: and it shall be given him."

There is an instructive Greek story which tells us of a noble youth who had a more than mortal guide. The Prince was frank and manly and docile; but on account of his inexperience often found himself in straits through which his own sagacity could not steer him. On such occasions, when in danger of falling into designing hands or committing himself to disastrous counsels, or when actually involved in distresses from which he could not extricate himself, this faithful friend was sure to speed to his rescue. Whatever was the scene of anxiety or affright, he had only to bethink himself of his kind and sagacious counsellor, and that moment Mentor was beside him. What Homer dreamed, the Gospel verifies. It tells that veiled from our view only by the curtain of this corporeal, but nearer to us than that flesh and blood which hides us from our truest selves, there is an ever-present friend who needs only to be remembered in order to prove a present help. It tells us that amidst all our embarrassments and sorrows, grief is never so near but deliverance is nearer still. And it tells us that all the confusion and blundering, the foolish bargains and infatuated proceedings which often make us so affronted or indignant at ourselves might all have been avoided had we timeously resorted to that wonderful Counsellor who encompasses all our ways. In other words, the Bible assures us that, however much we may suffer from the deficiency of our talents and the darkness of our understandings, we suffer still more from not taking advantage of that Wisdom from above who can enlighten our darkness and elevate all our powers. No man, by taking thought, can add a faculty to his mind any more than he can add a feature to his countenance or a cubit to his stature. But the man who has learned to pray, can, at the Throne of Grace, procure what really is the enhancement of his intellect, and the augmentation of his faculties; that Divine wisdom which will either supersede or supplement his own.

His must be a very easy calling who has never felt the need of more skill and prudence—more *wisdom* than is indigenous to himself. Take the most common instances. You are a father or a mother—perhaps a widowed father or a widowed mother. There are your children rising around you. Allowing that their minds are ever so susceptible and plastic, how important are your every movement and entire demeancur is their bearing on them! A single inconsistency, the most trivial inadvertency, coming with all the sanction of a parent's example, how influential for evil is it sure to be! How possible for a father, by mere inconsiderateness, to perpetuate his own worst qualities in the persons of many survivors; and, just because they loved him so well, and copied him so closely, how possible is it to transmit in his children's characters the facsimile of his *worser* self—the image of his frivolity, or peevishness, or indolence. Nay, how possible is it to convert a child into the perennial monument of a few occasional follies—to prolong, in its habitual character, the sayings and doings of a few unguarded moments! Then, again, there may be among these children more puzzling problems—some who are neither affectionate nor docile—who are not likely, by a mere moral imbibition, to take in the good influences with which they are surrounded —problems in whose management more than patience and tenderness is needful—refractory, selfish, or peculiar natures, on which nothing but the decisive measures of a deep-seeing sagacity— the bold strokes of a forceful nature—can make any permanent impression. Whosoever occupies a station of moral influence—a station where his labour lies amongst the most perilous materials with which man can intermeddle—the affections and dispositions—the *wills* of other people, must have amazing self-reliance, or a deplorable callousness, if he is not frequently crushed down by the solemnity of his position. It was by one in such a position that a most considerate and magnanimous prayer was offered—a prayer whose spirit every parent, and teacher, and pastor should emulate, just as a similar answer is what every parent, and teacher, and pastor who offers it is encouraged to expect:—" In Gibeon the Lord appeared to Solomon in a dream by night: and God said, 'Ask what I shall give thee.' And Solomon said, 'Thou hast showed unto thy servant David my father great mercy, according as he walked before thee in truth and in righteousness, and in uprightness of heart with thee: and thou hast kept for him this great kindness, that thou hast given him a son to sit on his throne as it is this day. And now, O Lord my God, thou hast made thy servant king instead of David my father; and I am but a little child: I know not how to go out or come in. And thy servant is in the midst of thy people which thou hast chosen, a great people, that cannot be numbered nor counted for multitude. Give, therefore, thy servant an understanding heart to judge thy people that I may discern between good and bad: for who is able to judge this thy so great a people? And the speech pleased the Lord that Solomon had asked this thing. And God said unto him, ' Because thou hast asked this thing, and hast not asked for thyself long life; neither hast asked riches for thyself, nor hast asked the life of thine enemies; but hast asked for thyself understanding to discern judgment; behold, I have done according to thy words: lo, I have given thee a wise and understanding heart, so that there was none like thee before thee, neither after thee shall any arise like unto thee. And I have also given thee that which thou hast not asked, both riches and honour.' "*

3. Is any among you embarked in an important undertaking? "Commit thy way unto the Lord, and He shall bring it to pass. In all thy ways acknowledge Him, and He will direct thy steps." Some feel as if it were presumption to implore God's blessing on their daily toils and secular callings. They feel as if spiritual mercies were the only proper themes for prayer, and as if it were a desecration of Jehovah's presence-chamber to carry thither matters so mean as our worldly undertakings and every-day concerns. And assuredly if a man were to make nothing else than his worldly welfare the subject of his supplications, it would be much the same with him as with those sordid spirits who had no other use for the Temple than to make it a market-place, and sell their oxen and doves; and "Let not that earthly-minded man think that he shall receive anything of the Lord." But if you be in the habit of resorting to the Throne of Grace for spiritual mercies, to that Throne you naturally and lawfully resort for temporal mercies also. And, indeed, no undertaking or employment of a Christian can be altogether secular. The mere fact that it is his gives it a certain sacredness, and identifies it with the interests of God's kingdom on earth. It is not a matter of no moment whether a servant who makes profession of religion shall fulfil the duties of his station no better than others who make no profession. It is not a matter of no religious moment whether a student pro-

* 1 Kings iii. 5--13

fessing piety shall not be more industrious and successful than one who scoffs at the Bible. And it is not a matter of no consequence whether the business transactions and household arrangements and personal exertions of Christian professors shall not surpass the usual style of the worldly. And so far as the glory of God and the honour of the Divine Redeemer are implicated, it is incumbent on every believer to bespeak from above that help which will make him more than a conqueror even in his worldly calling. But more than this: there is nothing which can be momentous to a child of God which is not also interesting to his Heavenly Father. A gentle parent is not only ready to snatch his child from the fire, but to relieve him from lesser miseries. He is not only willing to give him an ample education or provide for his distant well-being; but if there be nothing wrong in it, he is ready to indulge even his least desires—ready to help him in his most trivial pursuits. And so, the petition, "Our Father, who art in heaven—give us this day our daily bread," is to teach us that nothing affects the welfare or comfort of his feeblest child, but it is ready to receive the consideration of his Heavenly Father, and so is a fit subject for prayer. And just as the Lord is ready to hear prayer in such cases, so it is the wisdom of every one to lighten his own labour and secure his own success by timely supplication. Jacob's prayer did more to propitiate Esau than Jacob's present. Eliezer's petition, as he knelt by the camel's side, did more to prosper his embassy than his own and his master's precautions. And

Hezekiah's intercession rescued Jerusalem when its walls were of little use, and nothing but the arm of Jehovah could lay the invader low. We know not the secret history of this world's mightiest transactions and its proudest monuments; but from the little that we know we can affirm that the men who have prospered best are the men who have taken time to pray. It was to prayer that Henry IV. of France ascribed his crown, and Gustavus owed his victories. The father of the modern fine arts was wont, before he began any new composition, to invoke His inspiration, who in other days taught Aholiab; and the Goliath of English literature felt that he studied successfully when he had prayed earnestly. And what Michael Angelo and Milton and Johnson found so hopeful to their mighty genius cannot hinder us. You have read in our own history of that hero who, when an overwhelming force was in full pursuit, and all his followers were urging him to more rapid flight, coolly dismounted in order to repair a flaw in his horse's harness. Whilst busied with the broken buckle, the distant cloud swept down in nearer thunder; but just as the prancing hoofs and eager spears were ready to dash down on him, the flaw was mended, the clasp was fastened, the steed was mounted, and like a swooping falcon he had vanished from their view. The broken buckle would have left him on the field a dismounted and inglorious prisoner. The timely delay sent him in safety back to his huzzaing comrades. There is in daily life the same luckless precipitancy, and the same profitable delay The man who, from his prayerless waking, bounces off into the business of the day, however good his talents and great his diligence, is only galloping on a steed harnessed with a broken buckle, and must not marvel if in his hottest haste, or most hazardous leap he be left inglorious in the dust; and though it may occasion some little delay beforehand, his neighbour is wiser who sets all in order before the march begins.

4. But covet most earnestly the best gifts. Is any among you in earnest about his soul, but distressed by reason of darkness? " If ye being evil know how to give good gifts unto your children, how much more will your Heavenly Father give the Holy Spirit to them that ask him?" If any one be in the outset of his religious inquiries, he will feel a special lack. The subjects to which his thoughts are now turned are novel. Till now, he has not paid much attention to them, and now, when they have become urgent, he feels foreign in the midst of them. He takes up the Bible, but it is altogether so peculiar, the truths it handles are so far out of the ordinary way of his thinking, and its very style is so alien to his ordinary mode of expression, that he feels much as a person might be supposed to feel who had somehow been transported to another planet, and not only saw forms of existence there totally different from anything which his fancy had ever conceived, but who had not been long among them till he began to suspect that he was not competent to understand them thoroughly. He has not been long in this new world till he begins to suspect that more than five senses are needed

here. He notices appearances which indicate that matters are transpiring which his ear cannot detect, and into which his eye cannot penetrate. He finds himself in a world of deepest interest, but a world of distressing mystery. Enough comes within his cognizance to make him wish that he was able to know it all; but enough to convince him that its most characteristic things are those which he does not know, and has not the means for finding out. Or, to use a more obvious illustration: Most persons, in the outset of their spiritual enlightenment, are in the case of the blind man at Bethsaida when his sight was half restored. He looked up and saw men like trees walking. He saw that he was in a world of light, and verdure, and vivacity; but it was all a jumble of green men, and walking trees—a medley of light and motion. He had no clear perceptions—no sharp and definite ideas. But—another touch of the same miraculous finger!—he looked again, and the men walked and the trees stood still, the boats winged their limpid way over quivering Galilee, and lo! Bethsaida sleeping in the summer noon. At the commencement of a religious inquiry, the man finds himself in a region of deep interest, but withal, a region of dim outlines and flickering obscurity. His notions run into one another, and he has rather a confused impression of the extent of the landscape, than a clear perception of any one object in it. Like the man who confounded walking people with growing trees, he is apt to confound one doctrine with another. He mistakes faith for the Saviour. He blends together the

Gospel and the Law, and thinks that there must be a change in himself before he is entitled to believe in Christ for salvation. And if, at this stage, friendly counsellors come in with their distinctions and explanations, they answer much the same purpose as a neighbour who should have endeavoured to expound the landscape to the half-enlightened Galilean. After all his well-meant efforts, the scene would still have showed a medley of glimmering colours and dancing blotches, and nothing but another touch of the omnipotent hand could project the whole into splendid distinctness. And, just as in the case of the dim-seeing Galilean, it was not so much a sunshine as a ghost of light which saluted his eye-balls—so, in the outset of a spiritual earnestness, it is not the warm and radiant Gospel which glads the exploring vision, but a cold and hazy version of it. It is not a Gospel over which the love of God sheds its flood of endearment, but a Gospel in a mist—a Gospel of conflicting attributes and ambiguous meaning—a Gospel of dim love and doubtful kindness. And it is not till a power from on high imparts clearer perceptions and intenser vision that, like the joyful scenes which rushed on the fully-opened eyes of the Bethsaidan, the scheme of mercy stands out in assuring distinctness, and then melts in upon the soul in its genial beauty and overwhelming glories.

Now, my friends, if any of you are in this case—if you have for some time wished a clear theology and a soul-satisfying religion, this is the way to get it. You have, perhaps, sought it in books and in sermons. Perhaps you have sought it in the Bible, and in close thinking, and yet you have not found it. Seek it "from above." Seek it in prayer. Don't shut the Bible and forsake the sanctuary. Don't fling away the book, or cease to reflect and meditate, but seek the wisdom from on high. It is not plainer preaching—certainly it is not a clearer Bible that you need; but it is a clearer eyesight—a power of sharper discernment, and a more perspicacious insight in yourself. This " opening of your eyes "—this exaltation of your faculties, God alone can give. But he *will* give it. You lack wisdom. Ask it of God. With your reading, hearing, meditation, mingle prayer; and, in the brightening of your views, and the strengthening of your faith, you will find that God is sending out his light and truth, and, by the illumination of his own Spirit, is making you wiser than all your teachers.

LECTURE V.

THE OPEN REWARD OF SECRET PRAYER

'Thou, when thou prayest, enter into thy closet, and when thou hast shut thy door, pray to thy Father which is in secret; and thy Father which seeth in secret, shall reward thee openly."—MATT. vi. 6

WE do not need to enter the closet in order to find the Lord. He is ever near to us. But we enter it in order to escape from distractions, and in order to regain those associations, and, it may be, to surround ourselves with those mementos which we formerly found helpful to our prayers. One who has great powers of abstraction may take refuge from surrounding bustle in the depths of his own spirit, and pass along the crowded streets in the perpetual hermitage of his own self-seclusion, undiverted and undistracted by all that is whirling round him. But few have this talent of inward sequestration—this power to make a closet of themselves; and, in order to find for their thoughts a peaceful sanctuary, they must find for their persons a tranquil asylum. It little matters where or what it is. Isaac went out into the field, and Jacob plied his night-long prayer beside the running brook. Abraham planted a grove, and, in the cool shadow of his oaks at Beersheba, he called on the name of the

Lord. Abraham's servant knelt down beside his camel; and it would appear, from some of his psalms, that a cave, a mountain fastness, or a cavern in the rocks, was David's frequent oratory. Peter had chosen for his place of prayer the quiet and airy roof of his sea-side lodging, when the messengers of Cornelius found him. It would seem that the open air—the noiseless amplitude of the " solitary place "—the hill-side, with the stars above, and the shadowy world below—the fragrant stillness of the garden when evening had dismissed the labourers, were the places where the Man of Sorrows loved to pray. It was in the old church of Ayr that John Welsh was wont, all alone, to wrestle with the angel of the covenant; and we have stood in the wild rock-cleft where Peden found frequent refuge from his persecutors, and whence he caused his cry to ascend " unto the Lord most high." It does not need four walls and a bolted door to make a place of prayer. Retirement, and silence, and a sequestered spirit will create it anywhere. By the shore of the sounding sea—in the depths of the forest—in the remoteness of the green and sunny upland, or the balmy peacefulness of the garden bower—nay, amidst the dust of the dingy wareroom, or the cobwebs of the owlet-haunted barn—in the jolting corner of the crowded stage, or the unnoticed nook of the travellers' room, you have only to shut your eyes, and seclude your spirit, and you have created a closet there. It is a closet wherever the soul finds itself alone with God.

But, besides a still and silent place, it is important to have a stated place for prayer—" thy" closet—thy familiar and frequented place. Although places have not so much influence on us as persons, their influence is great. There are places where we would like to be when trial comes—places where we should like to be if we are to sicken and be laid aside—places where we should like to die—and places where we find it most congenial and delightful to pray. Homes of the spirit they are; places that seem to understand us and be in sympathy with us; places that have, as it were, imbibed, and do still retain, something of the joys we once tasted in them; places which make bereavement less awful, loneliness less desolate, happiness more intense, and heaven more near. When Elijah came to Sarepta, and found the son of the widow dead, he snatched the child from the bosom of the weeping mother and carried him " to the loft where he abode, and laid him on his own bed." And there " he cried unto the Lord, O Lord, my God, let this child's soul come into him again." He felt as if this loft, where he had so often prayed before, was the likeliest place for prayer now—the place where he might penetrate into Jehovah's nearest presence and procure an unprecedented blessing. And on this principle, perhaps, it was that David, when tidings came of the death of Absalom, hasted up to the " chamber over the gate." His heart was breaking, and lest it should split altogether in this unutterable sorrow, he sped away to the place where he had found lesser sorrows lightened; and, as he staggered up into this secret sanctuary, passionate grief began to give place to prayer, " O my son Absalom, my son, my son Absalom! would God I had died for thee, O Absalom, my son, my son!" And this is the best consecration any sanctuary or secret chamber can acquire—the consciousnesss that there you have met with God, and the hope instinctive that there you may meet him yet again. Happy are you if there be a house of prayer or a private dwelling which awakens in you, as you near it, a rush of holy feelings or happy recollections—a sanctuary round which a constant Sabbath shines and a perpetual air of heaven reposes. And happy are you if, in your residence, there be a room—however sombre the stranger may think it—which you cannot enter without a secret comfort suffusing your spirit; a room where, in dreariest moments, you feel that you are not friendless and in darkest days that you are not hopeless; a room in which memory has built its Peniels and Ebenezers—its memorials of ecstatic hours and answered petitions; a chamber which you abandon with regret when called to quit the dwelling, as if, in leaving it, you left the gate of heaven—the closet where you used to shut to the door and pray to your Father in secret, and feel that he was hearing you.

And here I may just notice, that besides the open return, there is a *secret* reward of secret prayer. There is a peculiar and present joy in communion with God. The deepest pleasures are the purest; and of all pleasures the purest is the peace of God. To feel that he is love—to draw so near him as to forget the world—so near as to lose the love of sin—so near that all sensual delights are drowned in the river of his pleasures, and all holy joys enhanced in the brightness of his smile—to bask, for ever so brief a moment, in the light inaccessible, and rejoice with loyalty of spirit in Jehovah's righteous sovereignty, and feel, through all recesses of the soul, the sin-supplanting flow and beatific thrills of infinite holiness and soul-transforming love—to be this, and feel this, is, of all pleasures the sweetest—of all blessedness the purest and most profound. And next to this high communion with God—next to this joy of passions lulled, and sins slain, and self-forgotten in adoring fellowship with the Father of Lights—is their sedater comfort who can pour their griefs into their Heavenly Father's bosom, or who feel that they have bespoken help against coming toils and trials at their Heavenly Father's hand. To know that God is near—to know that he is trusted, honoured, loved—to feel that you are acting towards him as a reverential and affectionate child, and that he is feeling towards you as a gracious and compassionate Father—there is in this, itself, an exquisite satisfaction, a present reward.

> The calm retreat, the silent shade,
>   With pray'r and praise agree;
> And seem by thy sweet bounty made
>   For those who follow thee.
>
> There, if thy Spirit touch the soul,
>   And grace her mean abode;
> Oh! with what peace, and joy, and love,
>   She communes with her God.

> There, like the nightingale, she pours
>   Her solitary lays;
> Nor asks a witness of her song,
>   Nor thirsts for human praise

But, besides this secret reward—this present recompense, of which the praying soul alone is conscious—there is an open reward of secret prayer promised in the text, and verified wherever secret prayer is practised.

1. And, first of all, we remark that the answer is sometimes open when the prayer is secret. The world sees the result when it little suspects the effectual antecedent. When Jacob and Esau met—on the one side the shaggy chieftain with his four hundred swordsmen, and on the other side the limping shepherd with his caravan of children and cattle—a flock of sheep approaching a band of wolves; when the patriarch took his staff in his hand and stepped forward to meet the embattled company, and the anxious retinue awaited the issue—they saw the tear start into the rough huntsman's eye—they saw the sword drop from Esau's hand—they saw his brawny arms round Jacob's neck—they saw in the red savage a sudden and unlooked-for brother. They saw the result, but they had not seen the prelude which led to it. They had not been with Jacob at the ford of Jabbok the night before. They had not viewed his agony and heard his prayer; and though they noticed the halting limb, they did not know the victory whose token it was. They saw the patriarch, the husband, and the father; but they knew not that he was a prince with God, and had gained Esau's heart

from him who has all hearts in his hand. The halting thigh and the pacified foe were obvious; but the wrestling overnight was unknown. The reward was open, but the prayer was secret.

And so there are many benefits which a believer secures by prayer—benefits which the world envies or wonders at, but of which the world knows not the secret source. "This man—there is some charm about him, for all things answer with him. Things in which others fail, he puts to his hand to them, and instantly they take another turn—they swing right—they stand fast—they prosper well. He has some magic—for whatever be the mischief, he escapes it—whatever be the calamity, it cannot come near him. He has got the talisman which made the wearer invisible, all except his shadow. When any disaster comes down, it crushes that shadow—any blow, it divides that shadow—any trap, it only catches that shadow,—his truest self gets always clear off." You are perfectly right. It is a singular fact—a peculiar circumstance. "He that dwelleth in the secret place of the Most High, shall abide under the shadow of the Almighty. He shall cover thee with his feathers, and under his wings shalt thou trust. Thou shalt not be afraid for the terror by night, nor for the arrow that flieth by day. A thousand shall fall at thy side, and ten thousand at thy right hand; but it shall not come nigh thee. Only with thine eyes shalt thou behold, and see the reward of the wicked. Because thou hast made the Lord, who is my refuge, even the Most High, thy habitation, there shall no evil befall thee, neither shall any plague come nigh thy dwelling. Thou shalt call upon him, and he will answer thee: he will be with thee in trouble. He will deliver and honour thee."* Prayer is the talisman. The secret of the Lord's presence is the protecting charm. The eye of Omniscience detects his dangers, and the hand of Omnipotence clears his path, and finishes his work, and dispels or reconciles his foes. The closet secured it, but the world beholds it. The prayer was secret but the reward is open.

Amongst these open rewards of secret prayer, we would specify presence of mind and composure of spirit. There are some persons of a calm temperament, who pass sedately through every scene, and are seldom taken by surprise. They are persons of ready wit and exhaustless resources and constant self-command. But there are others fearful and foreboding, easily stunned, and easily agitated. They are perpetually apprehending a lion in the street, and go about any new undertaking with as much anxiety as would suffice for the most arduous enterprise. They will pass by the perilous house on which they are plotting a visit, or at last address themselves to the knocker with as much trepidation as if they expected an ogre to dart from behind it. And when any little incident occurs—any conjuncture requiring promptitude or dexterity—their wits, only agile in forsaking them, are sure to be out of the way. The moment is flown—the propitious instant is past—and it is only when the opportunity is gone and for ever that the

* Psalm xci

perceive the very thing they should have said or done, but in their confusion it did not occur to them. For this sore evil we know no better remedy than the prescription of the text. Prayer calms and fortifies the mind, and so prepares it for the rapid incidents and sudden emergencies of the day. But it does more than this. Just as you may have noticed those who move in the highest circles, and who are accustomed to the loftiest society; they not only continue calm and collected when others are embarrassed or unhinged, but in circumstances of delicacy or distress to others, by a certain high-born address—a certain conscious felicity—they not only save themselves from awkwardness, but give a happy extrication to all around them. So there are certain persons belonging to the peerage of the faithful—men of as old a family as Enoch's—princely natures who are wont to converse even with the King of kings—men who in their walk with God have learned the happy art of possessing their own souls and tranquillizing the souls of others. Their hearts are fixed, and when they hear of evil tidings, they not only are not themselves afraid, but their assurance comforts and composes others. And beyond all this, the man of prayer is preternaturally prompted and strengthened from above. Like the first disciples, he needs to take no thought how or what he shall say or do, for in the hour of exigency the Holy Ghost will teach him. And hence, in all high conjunctures, men of prayer have surpassed themselves, and have felt that a courage, or prudence, or eloquence, was lent them, at which they themselves wondered, and which they only understood by recollecting that in their lack of wisdom they had asked of God. And so, brethren, if you would be carried bravely through scenes of affright—dexterously through scenes of difficulty—or triumphantly through scenes of awful alternative, resort to your Father in secret. When Nehemiah was enabled to put the case of his people so touchingly to the Assyrian monarch —the pathos of his statement—the unwonted kindness of the king—and the prompt concession of his prayer, were the open reward of a secret ejaculation.* And when Paul, on board the foundering ship, played such a gallant part—the prisoner superseding centurion, captain, pilot, and all—the heroic coolness, the veteran sagacity, and sublime composure which made him appear a sort of deity, were the answer to fasting and prayer. When his friends asked the great physician Boerhaave how he could possibly go through so much work from day to day, and pass tranquil through so many fretting scenes, he told them that his plan was to devote the first hour of every morning to prayer and meditation on the word of God.

Another open reward of secret prayer is spirituality of mind. By a spiritual mind we do not mean a severe mind, or a sombre. We do not mean a peculiar phraseology, or an affected religionism; but we mean that state of a mind right with God, when it is all alive to the things of God,—that vividness of faith when the things unseen are very solid, and that vivacity of feel-

* Nehemiah ii. 4—6

ing when things sacred are congenial and interesting and affecting. A spiritual mind is one to which the Bible is something better than a Dictionary, and to which the Sabbath, with its exercises, does not bring the sense of drudgery. It is a mind clear-seeing and keen-hearing; a mind of quick perceptions and prompt emotions; a mind to which the Saviour stands out a living person, and for which heaven is waiting an expected home: a mind so sensitive, that sin makes it writhe with agony, whilst it finds in holiness a true deliciousness, and in God's conscious favour an Elysian joy. Now, brethren, if you would possess such a mind you must keep it fresh and vegete and lifesome by secret prayer. Some professors are, in this respect, deplorably wanting. Their religion is formality. Their conversation rather quotes from past experience than utters what they now realize and feel. True piety is like the vestal fire, which was intended to burn day and night, and never to go out, and which never did go out, so long as they remembered to replenish it day by day. The religious profession of some people is like the yellow ashes on a key-cold altar, which show that there once were warmth and light and flame, but which also show that they have neglected it and suffered it to die. Brethren, do you, morning by morning, pour on the oil of secret prayer, and add the fresh fuel of some Bible-truth well pondered, and your fire will not go out. The altar of your heart will never subside to the clear-steel coldness which will make him who comes in contact with it shudder; and you will always have, at least, a little spark with which to kindle others Or, using a homelier metaphor, religion, in the soul of man, is like some precious thing in a vessel of ill-seasoned timber. Not only does the rough wear of this rude world sore batter it, but the burning sun of secularity, the glow of daily business, is enough to fill it full of flaws and fissures; and it is only by putting it to steep overnight in the pool of Siloah, that the chinks will close, and the cracked and leaky firkin be rendered fit for another morning's use. But the man who abounds in secret prayer will not only preserve his own vitality,—he will carry away from God's presence peace and joy and energy enough to make him a benefactor to others. A man, mighty in prayer, is a perpetual comfort,— a continual cordial in a world like this. When a prayerless professor tries to comfort the afflicted, he defeats his own well-meant efforts. When he enters the house of mourning, or sits down by the sick man's side, it is like a traveller coming in from a frosty atmosphere to the chamber of a nervous invalid. Though enveloped in frieze and in fur himself, he brings enough of winter in his clothes to make the poor patient chatter. But the man of prayer bears about with him a genial clime. Even in the dead season of the year, when frost is black and fields are iron, he carries summer in his person. "All his garments smell of myrrh and aloes and cassia." For his closet is the ivory palace,—the gay conservatory where flowers of paradise are blooming all the year. There is a gladness in his coming for he never comes alone. He carries his Saviour with him.

Then comes the crowning recompense,—the open reward of the great day. At that day no man will be saved for his prayers. It will be said to none, "You have been so holy and so devout, you have prayed so much, and laboured so hard, that on you the second death has no power." But though it is entirely and solely for the prayers,—the precious blood and perfect righteousness of God's dear Son,—that any soul can enter heaven; there will, at that disclosing day, be a rich reward of secret prayers. When every one receives the things done in his body, eminent intercessors will receive the final answer to the prayers of a life-time. Of many of the petitions offered now we know not what becomes. Some are for places far away; some for people whom we never see again; some for blessings which, if bestowed, we can never know it. But all these prayers are efficacious. If prayers of faith, they all have prevalency. They have effected something; and they are all *self-registering*. They go into the Book of Remembrance They keep account of themselves, or rather God keeps it, and when the great day comes round, and the throne is set, and the books are opened, it will be seen how much every Christian has prayed, what were the gifts he coveted most earnestly, and what were the petitions he urged most frequently. And strange things will come to light that day. Here is one who was never known on earth; perhaps in all the right-hand company none can recollect his name. He was very poor. He had no money to give to the cause of Christ,—hardly the two mites;—and he was very plain, simple, and unlearned. He could not express himself. But his name is Israel. He was a prince with God, and see how often he has prevailed. And here is another who was bed-rid many years, could not work could not visit, could not write,—but she could pray. And see what a benefactress she has been. See this long list of affectionate intercessions for her relatives and neighbours and friends; these many supplications for the Church and the world, for the unconverted, for Missions, for mourners in Zion! And see the answers! What a Dorcas she has been,—though she could make no garments for the poor! What a Phœbe, —though she could not stir a step! What a Priscilla,—though she could expound the way of God to few, for her prayers often did it all! And here is another. He had just escaped from Papal darkness, and was beginning to enlighten others, when he was put in prison, and after months of languishing he went up from Smithfield in his chariot of fire,—a martyr of Jesus Christ. He never preached. He was refused the use of ink and pen. He wrote nothing. He printed nothing. He spake to no one, for thick dungeon-walls enclosed him. But he prayed. From the height of his sanctuary the Lord looked down: he heard the groaning of this prisoner; and in the Reformation sent the answer.

LECTURE VI.

REASONS WHY PRAYER IS NOT ANSWERED.

"Ask, and it shall be given you."—MATT. vii. 7.
"Ye ask, and receive not, because ye ask amiss."—JAMES iv. 3.

SUPPOSE that a man takes up his pen and a piece of parchment, and writes on the top of it, "To the Queen's Most Excellent Majesty, the humble petition of So and so," but there he stops. He sits with the pen in his hand for half an hour, but does not add another word, then rises and goes his way. And he repeats this process day after day—beginning a hundred sheets of paper, but putting into them no express request; sometimes, perhaps, scrawling down a few sentences which nobody can read, not even himself, but never plainly and deliberately setting down what it is that he desires. Can he wonder that his blank petitions and scribbled parchments have no sensible effect on himself nor on any one besides? And has he any right to say, "I wonder what can be the matter. Other people get answers to their petitions, but I am not aware that the slightest notice has ever been taken of one of mine. I am not conscious of having got a single favour, or being a whit the better for all that I have written?" Could you expect it? When did you ever finish a petition? When did you ever despatch and forward one to the feet of majesty?

And so, my friends, there are many persons who pass their days inditing blank petitions—or rather petitionless forms of prayer. Every morning they bend their knee, and continue a few moments in the devotional attitude. They address themselves to the Heavenly Majesty. They call on the " great and dreadful name " of God, and they go over a few words and sentences, but such incoherent and unfelt sentences as the child who cannot write would scrawl upon a piece of paper. Or perhaps they say nothing. They leave it a perfect blank. And after this form of worship they go their way and wonder why their prayers are not heard. Other people get answers, but they are not conscious that any prayer of theirs has ever produced the least effect.

Now, of this we are very certain, that there is no prayer but *something comes of it*. Leaving out of view those vain and rambling repetitions —those empty words which constitute the entire devotions of some formalists—we are warranted by the word of God to aver that there is no real prayer which is not somehow disposed of—no request presented at the mercy-seat, which is not, in Bible language, " considered," and either refused or granted. Many appear to fancy that prayers are like a flight of promiscuous missiles, of which a few find the mark, but the greater number alight nowhere and bring back nothing.

This infidel and irrational view gets no countenance from the word of God. There we learn, that if it be a prayer at all—a sincere desire offered to the living God in his appointed way—it obtains an answer—whether that answer be a full or partial compliance, or an entire refusal. And it therefore becomes a question of the utmost practical moment to know what those conditions are that mar the efficacy, or impede the return of prayers.

1. It is competent to the sovereign to fix the channel through which he desires that his subjects should transmit their petitions. Owing to their elevated rank, some have a right to request an immediate audience of majesty, and present their applications in proper person and in their own name; but usually there is some fixed medium through which the suits of common subjects must come—a particular minister through whom all memorials and supplications must be transmitted. Now there is a celestial peerage who come before the King of kings in their own right. The sons of God—some orders of the heavenly host—need no mediator in drawing near to God. They come with veiled faces and lowly reverence, but still they come in virtue of their birth-right—they come direct. It is not so, however, with our world's population. Not so much on account of our lowlier rank, as of our personal demerit, there is no immediate entrance for any son of Adam into the presence of the heavenly majesty. But there is a day's-man appointed; and, so to speak, it is a standing order in the court of heaven, that each petition from

earth shall be transmitted through "the minister of the new covenant"—through that divine person on whose shoulder is devolved the government of this our far-off colony. Now, what say you? Suppose that any one should try to overleap this standing order—suppose that any one should either in his proud stubbornness scorn it, or in his carelessness forget it, and try to forward his petition in his own name—can he wonder if an omission so flagrant should ensure its rejection? The petition may be very earnest and its object may be perfectly right, but the mode of its transmission is wrong. And this is no matter of mere etiquette, like some of the court-arrangements of earth, but a matter of high import, and meant to fulfil exalted ends. It is designed in honour of the Prince of Peace, to whose memorable interposition it is owing that there is any loyalty in this revolted world, and to whose administration the entire of its affairs is now entrusted, and to whose name it is but seemly that every knee should bow. Whosoever would present an acceptable petition and secure a return to his prayer must remember that saying of the Lord Jesus himself, "Whatsoever ye shall ask the Father, in my name, that will I do, that the Father may be glorified in the Son."*

2. But, secondly, besides asking in a self-righteous spirit, a person may actually ask wrong things. A child who has never seen a serpent before and who looks at it through the glass-frame may think it very beautiful. As it curls and glides about in its folds of green and gold, and

* John xiv. 13.

its ruby eyes sparkle in the sun, it looks far prettier than more familiar objects, and the child may long to grasp it: "But what man is there among you who is a father, if his son ask a serpent, will he give him the serpent?" And supposing that the fretful child should weep because he is not allowed to fondle the asp, could worse befall him than just to be allowed to smash the case and clutch the envenomed reptile? The Lord has sometimes permitted his imperious and wayward children thus to punish themselves; but more frequently and more mercifully, he refuses their hearts' deceitful lust. One sets his eye on the golden serpent, and prays that God would make him rich. But the Lord still keeps the shining serpent beyond his reach; for should he have succeeded in hugging it to his bosom, it might have stung him with many sorrows, or even plunged him in perdition. Another sets his eye on the fiery flying serpent of fame, and wonders after it, and wishes that he too could fix his reputation to it, and see his own name flickering as a part of its meteor-train in its flight through the firmament. But this wish is also refused—and instead of a dizzy and dangerous renown, he is appointed to a safe obscurity. And sometimes requests, right or religious-looking, are refused. When the mother of Zebedee's children came and said, "Grant that these my two sons may sit, the one on thy right hand and the other on thy left, when thou comest in thy kingdom,"—there was a plausibility and a certain faith in the petition. It assumed that Christ had indeed a kingdom, and was yet to come gloriously, and it said that the highest honour she could seek for James and John, was the highest office there. But the request was ambitious. It was wrong and was refused.

3. And this leads us to remark that a person may ask right things with a wrong motive. When Simon Magus besought the Apostles that he might receive the gift of the Holy Ghost, he asked a good thing; emphatically the best thing; but he asked it with a bad motive, that he might make it a source of personal gain; and instead of a blessing his prayer was answered with a curse. " Ye ask and receive not, because ye ask amiss, that ye may consume it upon your lusts."* Even spiritual mercies are refused to you, because you would employ them on carnal ends.

4. Such a sin may be cherished in the heart as makes prayer unavailing. " If I regard iniquity in my heart, the Lord will not hear me."† To keep a sin in the heart whilst there is a prayer on the lips, is like going into the monarch's presence arm in arm with a rebel, or getting some noted enemy of his to countersign our petition. It is, as it were, courting a refusal. " It is effectually saying to God, 'Thy greatest blessing I am content to want. Holiness, deliverance from sin, I am willing to do without; but this particular boon, as it is thine to bestow, so I am reluctantly constrained to ask it from thee.' "‡ It is as if the one hand held out a plea for God's favour, and the other a plea for God's frown. In truth, it is the more honest part of the man contradicting the other; the sinner shouting *Nay* to

* James iv. 3.   † Psalm lxvi. 18.   ‡ Foster, M.

the *Amen* of the hypocrite, and drowning in his louder voice the feeble muttering of the feigned lips. You have all heard of Augustine's prayer. In the days of his licentiousness he had too much conscience to live without prayer, and too much love of sin to pray without a secret reservation; and so his prayer ran, "Lord convert me—oh, convert me—but not to-day, Lord, not to-day." And the same is the translated purport of many a prayer One prays, "Lead me not into temptation," when he has already in his possession the play-house ticket which he means to use that evening; or when he has already made an engagement with some of his ungodly friends, and is looking forward with eagerness to their society. Another prays, "And forgive me my trespasses," when he has in his heart a scheme of revenge, and is already in imagination glorying over his humbled rival or his defeated adversary. And a third prays, "Lord, let me die the death of the righteous," when he has already made all the arrangements for some nefarious transaction, and when the very next act of self-denial which he is called to exercise will be the triumph of sensuality or self-indulgence. And a fourth cries, "As I to others mercy show I mercy beg from heaven;" and at that moment he is allowing some necessitous kinsman to languish in neglected misery or with an ample fortune is contributing nothing to the diffusion of that Gospel, which is the only means of rescuing men from eternal ruin.

5. Some prayers are not heard because men do not believe that God will grant them. Were you writing a note to a friend, and saying, "I

would be much the better for such a thing "— naming it. " You can easily spare it, but I have little expectation that you will do me such a favour." Would this be a likely way to compass his object? Though he had wished to fail, could he have worded his application otherwise? And so, when a man gets down on his knees and prays for pardon of his sins, or for the teaching of the Holy Spirit, or for assurance of salvation, but prays for them as if the Lord would grudge to give them, can he wonder that he is not heard? Whatsoever the Lord has promised, that he is willing to bestow, and " whatsoever things we ask in prayer, believing that we have them, we receive them."

6. Some prayers are not answered because, though earnest at the time, the petitioner has grown indifferent afterwards.

7. Some prayers are answered, but the answer is a long time arrived before the petitioner adverts to it. Like a man who despatches for the physician one express after another, and at last he arrives, and is actually in the house; but unapprised of his presence, the sick man sends off another messenger to hasten his approach. Or as you may have sent for some book or other object which you were anxious to possess, but as it is long of making its appearance, your anxiety to see it begins to abate, and by-and-bye you have almost forgotten it; when some day you take up a parcel that has long lain unopened in a corner of the room, and find that it is the very thing you were once so impatient to get. " And when did this arrive?" Oh! months ago. " How strange,

then, that I should never have noticed it till now!" In extreme agony Jacob vowed a vow, and prayed a prayer: "If God will be with me, and will keep me in this way that I go, and will give me bread to eat and raiment to put on, so that I come again to my father's house in peace; then the Lord shall be my God, and this stone which I have set up for a pillar shall be God's house." It was an earnest and importunate prayer. It was answered. Every petition was fulfilled. All that he asked, Jacob obtained. He got bread to eat; he got raiment to put on. He was delivered from Esau his brother. He came back to his father's house in peace, and in unimagined prosperity. But it never occurred to Jacob that his prayer was answered till the Lord himself reminded him. He might have seen the answer in his peaceful tent, in his grazing flocks and herds, in his large and powerful family, and in himself—the fugitive lad come home a prince and a patriarch. But it was not till the Lord appeared and said, "Arise, go up to Bethel, and dwell there; and make there an altar unto God that appeared unto thee when thou fleddest from Esau thy brother;" it was not till then that Jacob recollected the vow, or detected the answer; and had the Lord not reminded him, Bethel and its pillar might have faded for ever from Jacob's memory. And so, parents in the days of their children's infancy often pray for their children's conversion, and when they see their wayward freaks and wicked tempers, the tear starts in their eye, and they are ready to give up hope. But one by one the Lord brings them to himself. The prayer is partly or wholly answered, and ere they are gathered to their fathers, these parents find themselves surrounded by a godly seed. But it never strikes them that here is an answer to prayer. Or a company of Christians pray for a revival of religion, and they fix their eye on a particular spot of the horizon, nothing doubting but that it is there the cloud must appear. And whilst they kneel and pray and mourn that the sky continues brass, they never notice that in the opposite quarter the heavens are melting, and there is an abundance of rain. Though not in the form nor in the direction which they first desired, still the blessing is come, and perhaps in measure it surpasses their fondest expectation and their largest prayer.

10*

LECTURE VII.

CONFESSION, ADORATION, AND THANKSGIVING.

"I said, I will confess my transgressions unto the Lord and thou forgavest the iniquity of my sin.

"Be glad in the Lord, and rejoice, ye righteous: and shout for joy, all ye that are upright in heart." PSALM xxxii. 5. 11.

ALTHOUGH prayer, in its strictest sense, be the supplication of mercies for ourselves or others, the devotional exercises of believers are not confined to mere petitions. In the Psalms, and other Bible-specimens of prayer, we find acknowledgments of sin, the praises of the divine perfections, and grateful ascriptions for good and perfect gifts bestowed; and, that our survey may be the more complete, we shall bestow the present discourse on the three-fold subject of Confession, Adoration, and Thanksgiving.

CONFESSION.

There are three things which often hinder confession—callousness, sullenness, and remorse. In the anguish of newly-committed sin, or in the despair of a newly-awakened conscience, the guilt is so ghastly that the soul is afraid to approach it, even with a view to confession. Such was the Psalmist's case. His convictions were so dreadful that he wished some time to elapse, trusting that the interval might make it somewhat better. He " kept silence;" but, like the damper, which only makes the furnace draw the fiercer, the fire kindled in his spirit flamed the more furiously from his efforts to suppress it. He kept silence, but, whilst he did so, his bones waxed old, and his moisture was turned into summer's drought. But, after thus battling with his agonies, he yielded. In a lull of this mental fever—in a lucid interval of his remorseful frenzy, he took another thought, and said, " I will confess my transgressions unto the Lord;" and no sooner said than there was a great calm in his spirit. His sin was confessed; his trespass was forgiven; his convictions vanished; the Lord's hand withdrew; and, in the gayety of his convalescent spirit, he began to sing, " Blessed is he whose transgression is forgiven, whose sin is covered."—Then, there are others, who, without anything of the Psalmist's sharp remorse, have a sullen sense of wrong. They know that they have offended, and that there is an unsettled controversy betwixt themselves and God; but, instead of resorting at once to his mercy in Jesus Christ, they wish to wear off their guilt by degrees They would like to work it off, or live it off. They expect that its crimson hue will fade in the course of time, and that its pricks will be blunted in the lapse of years; and, as they cannot brook to assume the publican's attitude, or to come as poor abjects to the fountain, they carry their sin about with them, unacknowledged and unconfessed. Perhaps they go again and again to prayer; but there is no confidence in their worship, and no earnestness in their petitions, for this sin is constantly presenting itself, and they are as constantly evading it. They are walking contrary to God, and he walks contrary to them. Feeling that their position is false, their air is embarrassed and uneasy. Their footing is insecure, and their resistance to temptation feeble. And, going about their daily occupations under the Lord's frown they are constantly frustrated. Perhaps their worldly business goes back; most probably they are getting into endless perplexities and entanglements—vexing their friends when they did not mean to offend them—lowering themselves in the eyes of others when they did nothing particularly wrong: and standing ruefully, because remorsefully amid the wreck of many schemes, and the crash of many efforts; and proving by a costly experiment, the truth of the saying—" He that covereth his sins shall not prosper." Oh! that they were wise enough to turn round and prove the truth of that other alternative—" But whoso confesseth and forsaketh them shall have mercy."—And then, again, there are some who are kept from confessing their sin, neither by the violence of their remorse, nor the sullenness of their spirits, but by the callousness of their conscience. They have got so much into the custom of sinning without compunction, that they can scarcely understand how confession could bring them any relief, or make them happier than they this moment are. A man who has laboured under a disease for many years comes at last to lay his account with it. If he has no stound of exquisite anguish, or no unusual feeling of pain or debility—if he be in his " frail ordinary"—he is content. He expects no better. The truth is, his nervous system has become inured to a certain amount of habitual suffering, and disease itself ceases to be pain. But if some feat of medicine, or some sudden miracle should expel the ailment from his system, and give him at once absolute soundness, he would perceive a world-wide difference betwixt the dull apathy of disease and the joyous gush of health—betwixt mere exemption from torture and positive sensations of salubrity and vigour. " By habit in sin the stings of remorse may be blunted, yet peace never will return. By repeating transgression a great many times, we all come at last to feel a general and settled uneasiness of heart, which is a constant burden, but so constant that the sinner comes to consider it as a necessary part of his existence ; and when, at last, he comes and confesses his sins, and finds peace and happiness, he is surprised and delighted with the new and strange sensation." *

Were confession a mere act of self-mortification—did it end in mere regrets and self-reproaches—it would answer little end. The rash words which no compunction can recall—the wasted Sabbaths which no wishes can redeem— the broken hearts of distant days and departed friends, which no churchyard sighs can heal, and the demolished joys which no tears can create anew:

* Abbot's " Young Christian."

> For violets pluck'd, the sweetest showers
> Can ne'er make grow again :

were confession merely the mental penance of remembering and brooding over these, there were no need to add it to the sum of human sorrow. But evangelical confession—that discovery and acknowledgment of the outstanding sins of his history, and the conspicuous sins of his character, as well as of the guilt of his original—which the Word of God requires from each of us, is for purposes totally different. Evangelical confession is the inlet to peace with God, and the outset of new obedience.

The great object of self-examination should be to search out the sin with the express view, and on very purpose, to cast it into the sin-cancelling Fountain opened in the House of David; and then the confession will bring comfort to the sinner, when he thinks that the cleansing currents of atoning blood have washed his guilt away. Like the camp of Israel on the day of atonement. They all met—the most solemn fast of their year—before the tabernacle, in the morning very early; and after many other ceremonies, two goats were brought up to the high-priest at the altar. He placed himself between them, and shook a box, in which were two little tablets, one inscribed. "For Jehovah," the other, "For Azazel." When he drew the one, he said with a loud voice, " For Jehovah," and placed the tablet on the head of the right-hand goat. Then he confessed over it his own and the people's sins, and slew it, and carried the blood into the Holy Place as an atonement for his own sins and the people's. The high-priest then went to the goat "Azazel,' and put his hands upon its head and confessed over it again the sins of himself and the people; and, when this was done, an appointed person came forward and carried the goat away to the wilderness, where it should wander and be lost, or threw it over the rocks that it might return no more. It needed the two-fold emblem to shadow Him whose atonement is at once the *removal* of guilt and the *reparation* for it;—whose blood cleanseth from sin, and whose worthiness carrieth sin away. And, just as the believing Israelite who could see the Lord's meaning in the touching token—as that Israelite would accompany, with earnest heart, the priest as he made confession over the victim's head, and would feel that his guilt was figuratively transferred to this innocent substitute; so, brethren, it is for us to confess our trespasses over His head who is the propitiation for the sins of the world, and on whom the Lord hath really laid the iniquities of us all. And if we do this—if we make the deliberate transference of our guilt to this all-sufficient substitute—like the Israelite who saw the trickling blood of the one victim, and felt, " Surely there is a sacrifice for sin. Let this blood be for mine;" so, looking to the wounded, dying Surety, we can securely feel, " This is not the blood of bulls or of goats, but a better sacrifice. This is the precious blood of God's only and well-beloved Son, shed for many. Let it flow for me. Jesus, be thou my righteousness—be thou the reparation for my sin." And then as the Israelite saw the strong man leading the other goat away into the wilderness, and gazed with interest after them till they disappeared in the grey horizon, and felt, " There the sin is away into a land not inhabited. It is lost —forgotten; if sought for it cannot again be found." So, if you sincerely transfer your sin to the Saviour, the Lamb of God will take it away. It will vanish from God's sight. It will be counted as if it had never been. You will be dealt with not only as one who has made expiation, but as one in whom there is no iniquity. You will be, in God's sight, as innocent; and that sin will never be punished in you which the Son of God hath atoned for, and which the Lamb of God hath taken away.

ADORATION.

The heart is the noblest part of human nature, and God says, " My son, give me thine heart." And, just as the affections are the noblest ingredient in human nature, so the elevation and the happiness of a human being mainly depend on the right bestowment and ample exercise of these affections. To be self-sufficient and self-seeking —that is, to keep all the affections to one's self —is the meanest and most miserable predicament a *creature* can be in. The homestead of a finite spirit—much more the desolate chamber of a sinful heart—does not contain resources enough for its own blessedness. The soul must go out from itself if it would find materials of joy. It must love its neighbour, or it must love the works of God, or it must love its family, or its circle of friendship, if it would not be absolutely dreary and forlorn And just as the soul's happiness depends on going *out* from itself, so its elevation depends on its going *up*—depends on its setting its affections on something higher than itself—something nobler, or holier, or more engaging.

The main part of true religion is the right bestowment of the affections. When these are set on the things above—on God and on Jesus who sitteth at God's right hand—they are set as high as a seraph can set his. They are set so high that they cannot fail to lift the character along with them, and make his a peculiar life whose ends in living are so lofty. A self-forgetting devotion to some noble earthly character has exerted a refining and elevating influence on many. Veneration for some illustrious sage has sometimes quickened a sluggard into a scholar, and enthusiastic attachment to a high-souled patriot has been known to kindle up an idler into a hero. But there is only One of character so lofty, and of influence so transforming, that love to Him will convert a sinner into a saint. Such a One, however, there is, and it is the business of the Gospel to make Him known.

When required to love the Lord with all their heart and soul and strength and mind, many feel as if they were asked to perform an impossibility. So vague, in general, are their notions of the Great Jehovah, that they feel much the same as if they were asked to love the principle of gravitation, or as if they were bidden bestow all their heart and mind on a fixed star, or as if they were invited to lay up treasure in a cloud, or told to set their affections on infinite space. I appeal to yourselves, Have not many of you felt something of this sort? The command, "Thou shalt love the Lord thy God with all thine heart," has it not often fallen on your ear in comfortless tones, rather as the funeral knell of your earthly affections than as the joyous summons to a present and attainable blessedness? Have you not rather felt it as a command to kill your earthly delights, than as an invitation to superadd a delight beyond them all? Have you not felt that the nearest approach to obedience you could make would be to cut the cords that bind you to the earth in sunder, and, seeing that you cannot love One so utterly beyond your conceptions, that you had better cease to love altogether?

This is the tendency of some books and systems. To love an abstract and impersonal God is Platonism. It is mysticism; but it is not Christianity. The God whom the Gospel bids us view, and whom Jesus bade us love, is not a distant power nor a dim abstraction. He is not a mere presence, nor a mere principle. He is not the most vague of all diffusions, and the most general of all general laws. But he is "the living God"—of all beings the most truly living—possessing, in intensest measure, all that is truly excellent and which has won our veneration in our fellow-men; combining in himself all that goodness which has ever arrested, or affected, or entranced us in the objects of our earthly admiration; not only wiser than the wisest, but more loving than the most affectionate—taking a kinder and wiser interest in us than the friend to whom, perhaps, we have devoted our earthly all, and more present with us than the most anxious friend can be. This Living God—possessing perfections at whose outburst the eye of an archangel dazzles—possesses also that power of special condescension and individual interest which can make him, to any one, most truly a friend and a perfect brother. If you be on a right footing with Him—a footing of friendship and loyalty —he is omnipotent and able to devote the same regard to all your interests as if immensity contained nothing else to attract his notice. He is omniscient, and able to keep you more constantly in his eye, and bear you more continually in his loving thoughts, than you are able to watch over the child, or to think of the friend, that is dearest. And though he be a consuming fire—though there be that in his holiness which is burning antipathy to sin—there is nothing in this holiness to hinder the humble soul from reposing on his faithfulness as securely as meekest brow ever rested on the fondest father's bosom. In the only aspect in which mortal eye can view him—in the person of Immanuel—the Living God draws near and says, " Thou shalt love the Lord thy God with all thy heart and with all thy soul and with all thy strength and with all thy mind." Thou shalt love—not Fate—not Providence—not Eternity—not Immensity—not Goodness—it is not even said the Deity—but " Thou shalt love the Lord thy God"—the God of the Bible—the great I Am—the Living God—Jehovah—the most majestic yet most loving and most lovely of all beings—thou shalt love the Lord with all thy soul. Love Him of whom the earth saw, not merely a living, but an incarnate, specimen in the person of Jesus Christ.

Whatever Platonists and mystics and transcendentalists may pretend to the contrary, and whatever a theology, tinctured by these human notions, may daily teach, if we would love God at all, we must look to the God of the Bible. It may be difficult to love the "First Cause" of the philosophers, or the Divine Essence of the schoolmen, or the far-off abstraction of the mystics,—but to love Immanuel, God with us, surely this is possible. By the door of the incarnation to get into some knowledge of God, and so into some love,—surely this is possible. To perceive the friendly disposition of the High and Holy One, even towards our wretched and guilty selves, is possible, when we look to the co-equal Son pouring out his blood a ransom for many. To apprehend his gentle and benignant bearing towards his own is easy when we look at John on the bosom of Jesus—yes, John on the bosom of God. And to see how much, not only of awful majesty and spotless sanctity, but how much of genial goodness and sweetest loveliness, how much of truest tenderness and heart-attracting graciousness there was in the Son of Mary, and yet doubt whether the living God be worthy of our love; dear brethren, which of you will answer,—This is possible? "That which was from the beginning, which we have heard, which we have seen with our eyes, which we have looked upon, and cur hands have handled of the Word of Life, (for the life—the Living One—was manifested, and we have seen him,' that which we have seen and heard declare we unto you, that ye also may have fellowship with us, and truly our fellowship is with the Father, and with his Son Jesus Christ. And these things write we unto you, that your joy may be full."

It is a simple truth,—but oh! that its starry letters sparkled in every eye,—would that its daily echo haunted every ear. The Incarnation is as truly our door of entrance into all true knowledge of God as the Atonement is our passport to heaven. The living person of Jesus is our theology as truly as the finished work of Jesus is our righteousness. We can reach no heaven except that which Immanuel bought for us, and we can know nothing of God except that which Immanuel is to us. But all that Immanuel was or is, all this the ever-blessed Godhead is; and ours is New-Testament divinity and ours is Christian worship, when in Jesus Christ we recognize " The Alpha and Omega, the beginning and the ending, which is, and which was, and which is to come, the Almighty."

And having discovered,—so far as finite powers and this dim world admit of,—what the true God really is, cultivate each reverent and trustful and admiring disposition toward him. Study his perfections on very purpose to enkindle praise, and when any fair scene in creation makes your heart right glad, or when any marvellous event in Providence solemnizes your spirit, let the thought of the Omnipotent creator and ruler convert it into present adoration. In the various revolutions of your worldly lot, and the changeful moods of feeling, let the recollection of the Divine perfections and recourse to the living God, be the instant asylum of your soul. Are you weary with the world's boisterousness—with the rough and high-handed ways of ungodly men? Seek the calm sanctuary of God's own presence. "Though a host encamp against me, one thing have I desired of the Lord—that will I seek after; that I may dwell in the house of the Lord all the days of my life, to behold the beauty of the Lord, and to inquire in his temple. For in the time of trouble he shall hide me in his pavilion; in the secret of his tent shall he hide me." Are you damped by the disappointment of some hope, or the downfall of some joy which you have long been rearing? Think of the permanence of God and the perpetuity of those joys which are at his own right hand, and in which he himself is part; and learn to build your blessedness on the Rock of Ages. Are you shut out from engagements which once were very sweet —society, recreations, and pursuits, in which you could indulge without satiety, and with ever-growing zest? Learn to live upon God, and like the prisoner of the Lord who beguiled her ten years' captivity with psalms, and who declares that the heavenly society of her cell made "its stones look like rubies,"* try to sing:

> How pleasant is all that I meet,
>   From fear of adversity free,
> I find every sorrow made sweet,
>   Because 'tis assigned me by thee.

* Madame Guion.

Thy will is the treasure I seek,
  For thou art as faithful as strong;
There let me, obedient and meek,
  Repose myself all the day long.

My spirit and faculties fail;
  Oh! finish what love has begun.
Destroy what is sinful and frail,
  And dwell in the soul thou hast won.

Oh, glory! in which I am lost,
  Too deep for the plummet of thought
On an ocean of Deity toss'd,
  I am swallow'd, I sink into nought

Yet lost and absorbed as I seem,
  I chant to the praise of my King;
And though overwhelmed by the thought,
  Am happy whenever I sing.

Do you grieve for the fickleness of man and mourn over friendships which have dried like summer-brooks? If the fault be not your own, think of the unchanging friend whose mercy is in the heavens and whose kindness is unaffected by the influences which make such havoc in the affections of earth. Do you feel the flesh fading? Then say, " Whom have I in heaven but thee? and there is none upon earth that I desire beside thee. My flesh and my heart faileth; but God is the strength of my heart and my portion for ever." Do you begin to wonder what is to become of your own mouldered dust and that of many dear to you, when long ages have slipped away and the inscription on your tomb is a dead language? Do not err, forgetting the Scriptures. Think of the great power of God. Remember who hath said, " I am the Resurrection and the

Life; he that believeth in me, though he were dead, yet shall he live." And thus, whatever be the grief, the vacancy, or fear, learn to find the antidote in GOD.

THANKSGIVING.

Adoration is devout meditation on what Jehovah *is*,—the praise of the divine perfections. Thanksgiving is delighted meditation on what the Lord has *done* for us or others—praise for his mercies. Such praise is " comely." Just as there is meanness in constant murmuring, so there is a gracefulness and majesty in habitual gratitude. And it is "pleasant." It is not the full purse or the easy calling, but the full heart, the praising disposition, which makes the blessed life; and of all personal gifts that man has got the best who has received the quick-discerning eye, the promptly-joyful soul, the ever-praising spirit.

And, my dear friends, in searching for the materials of gratitude, you have not far to go. If you have a lawful pursuit—a business to which, with a clear conscience, you can devote your energy—and a possession which raises you above the woes of penury; if you have contentment within, and affection around, you are a wealthy and a favoured man. Your daily lot may well be your daily wonder; and when other texts are exhausted you may find a theme for thanksgiving in your very home—a Hosannah in the blazing hearth and a *Jubilate* in each joyful voice and merry sound that echoes through your dwelling. But there are signal mercies, memorable interpositions and marvellous deliverances, which should be signalized by memorable thanksgivings. Remarkable interpositions are rare, but that life is rarer in which there has been no remarkable rescue; no signal interposition of Providence. Just see. Is there any one here present whose life has moved so smoothly that no accident ever endangered it, and that he cannot quote the time when there was but a hair-breadth betwixt him and death? The boat was upset, but you were saved. You intended going by the vessel that foundered at sea, but were unaccountably hindered. You passed along, and three seconds afterwards the tottering wall crashed down. You still preserve the hat that was grazed by the bullet, or the book that received the shot instead of yourself. And how did you feel at the time? When you fell from the precipice, or were thrown headlong from your startled steed, and rose uninjured, did all your bones say, Who is like unto thee, O Lord? When you just escaped the fatal missile, was gratitude to your gracious Preserver your first emotion, or did you merely thank your stars and congratulate yourself on your singular luck? And when the active arm saved you from drowning, or from being crushed to death in the crossing, when deposited on the place of safety you were pale, or you laughed wildly, or you clung to the arm of your deliverer, for the danger was dreadful; but have you since praised the Lord for *his* goodness, and for his wonderful work in saving you then? And do you adoringly remember it still?

"Whoso is wise, and will observe these things, even they shall understand the loving-kindness of the Lord."

Then, farther, there are moral perplexities and painful dilemmas; times of heart-trouble and fearful foreboding, followed by times for thanksgiving. "I love the Lord because he hath heard my voice and my supplications. The sorrows of death compassed me, and the pains of hell gat hold upon me: I found trouble and sorrow. Then called I upon the name of the Lord; O Lord, I beseech thee, deliver my soul. Gracious is the Lord and righteous; yea, our God is merciful. I was brought low, and he helped me. Return unto thy rest, O my soul, for the Lord hath dealt bountifully with thee. For thou hast delivered my soul from death, mine eyes from tears, and my feet from falling." You were in some desperate crisis of your history, and unless the Lord had made bare his mighty arm you saw nothing for it but disaster, confusion, and disgrace. But in that vale of Achor the Lord opened a door of hope. He raised up friends unlooked-for, or sent supplies unhoped-for, and step by step he opened up a gentle path, till you found yourself in a large place, and at gladsome liberty. And "what shall I render unto thee, O Lord, for all his benefits toward me? I will take the cup of salvation, and call upon the name of the Lord. I will pay my vows unto the Lord now, in the presence of all his people. I will offer to thee the sacrifice of thanksgiving, and will call upon the name of the Lord."

And the crowning mercies—the sweetest and

the surest—the most precious and most lasting—have you tasted spiritual mercies? "Then blessed be the God and Father of our Lord Jesus Christ, who hath blessed us with all spiritual blessings in Christ: according as he hath chosen us in him before the foundation of the world, that we should be holy and without blame before him in love." Have you heard of the Saviour? Then "Thanks be to God for his unspeakable gift." Have you found the pardon of sin? Then " Bless the Lord, O my soul, and forget not all his benefits, who forgiveth all thine iniquities; who as far as the east is from the west, so far hath removed my transgressions from me." Have you the lively hope to light you on your way through life? " Then blessed be the God and Father of our Lord Jesus Christ, who according to his abundant mercy hath begotten me again unto a lively hope by the resurrection of Jesus Christ from the dead, to an inheritance incorruptible, reserved in heaven for me." Have you found the promises fulfilled? " Blessed be the Lord that hath given rest unto his people, according to all that he promised. There hath not failed one word of all his good promise." Have you received an answer to your prayers? " I will praise thee, for thou hast heard me, and art become my salvation. I called upon the Lord in distress: the Lord answered me and set me in a large place. O give thanks unto the Lord, for he is good: for his mercy endureth for ever." It is written of that seraphic Christian, Joseph Alleine, " Love and joy and a heavenly mind were the internal part of his religion, and the large and fervent praises of God and thanksgiving for his mercies, especially for CHRIST, and the SPIRIT, and HEAVEN, were the external exercises of it. He was not negligent in confessing sin, but praise and thanksgiving were his natural strains; his longest, most frequent, and hearty services. He was no despiser of a broken heart, but he had attained the blessing of a healed and joyful heart." And this is indeed the most blessed life,—the most uplifted—the most impressive, and most heavenly. The Lord wills his people to be happy. He has provided strong consolation for them, and he desires that their enraptured praises and joyful lives should speak good of his name. Dear brethren, aspire at habitual thankfulness. Covet earnestly a life of prevailing cheerfulness and praise. Seek to have your souls often brimming over with holy gladness. Bring them into broad contact with every happy thing around you—not with every mad and foolish thing—but with everything on which God's countenance shines, and in which his joy-awakening Spirit stirs. Rejoice with a rejoicing universe. Rejoice with the morning stars, and let your adoring spirit march to the music of the hymning spheres. Rejoice with the jocund spring in its gush of hope and its dancing glory—with its swinging insect-clouds, and its suffusion of multitudinous song—and rejoice with golden autumn as he rustles his grateful sheaves, and claps his purple hands, as he breathes his story of fruition, his anthem of promises fulfilled—as he breathes it softly in the morning stillness of ripened fields, or flings it in Æolian sweeps from lavish orchards and branches tossing bounty into mellow winds. Rejoice with infancy as it guesses its wondering way into more and more existence, and laughs and carols as the field of pleasant life enlarges on it, and new secrets of delight flow in through fresh and open senses. Rejoice with the second youth of the heaven-born soul—as the revelations of a second birth pour in upon it, and the glories of a new world amaze it. Rejoice with the joyful believer when he sings " O Lord, I will praise thee : though thou wast angry with me, thine anger is turned away and thou comfortest me. Behold God is my salvation." Rejoice with him whose incredulous ecstasy has alighted on the great Gospel-secret—whose eye is beaming as none can beam save that which for the first time beholds the Lamb—whose awe-struck countenance and uplifted hands are evidently exclaiming, " This is my beloved, and this is my friend." Rejoice with saints and angels, as they rejoice in a sight like this. Rejoice with Immanuel, whose soul now sees of its travail. Rejoice with the ever-blessed Three, and with a heaven whose work is joy. **Be glad in the Lord, and rejoice, ye righteous; and shout for joy, all ye that are upright in heart.**

LECTURE VIII.

BIBLE INSTANCES.

" The effectual fervent prayer of a righteous man availeth much."—JAMES v 16.

Some have no turn for poetry, and others have no taste for science. Many have no aptitude for argument and dissertation, and no comprehension for abstract statement. But almost all men have an avidity for history. And what is history? It is truth alive and actual—truth embodied—truth clothed in our kindred clay. It is knowledge, not afloat on the mist-bounded sea—the shoreless abyss of speculation—but knowledge coasting it in sight of the familiar landmarks of time and place; knowledge anchored to this human heart, and coming ashore on this our every-day existence. It is the maxim of the book made interesting—the lesson of the pulpit or the desk made simple and delightful, by being read anew in living men. It is the grace made lovelier, and the attainment made more hopeful, by its exhibition in men of like passions and like affections with ourselves. The human spirit craves for history, and the Bible meets this craving. The half of it is history; and we shall devote this morning to some names of prayerful renown—Bible instances, and their modern parallels.

1. The first we quote is ENOCH. He walked with God. The conception we form of him, from what the Bible tells us, is, that his was a life of delightful communion and constant devotion. He had discovered the living God, and, from the moment of that discovery, could date his blessed life. So correct was his view of the Divine character, that he was irresistibly drawn toward it in confidence and love. So vivid was that view that he never forgot it, and so influential that it completely altered him. He "came to God;" "he walked with God;" and "he pleased God." "Every sacred engagement was performed with a holy alacrity. Every call to worship welcomed as it came, from its inviting him to contact with 'the Father of Spirits.' Every excursion of sanctified thought—every emotion of virtuous feeling—was sustained and encouraged, in anticipation of this intercourse, or as the result of its enjoyment. 'God was in all his thoughts.' If he looked upon the heavens, he was there; if he contemplated the earth, he was there; if he retired into his own bosom, he was there. He felt his presence pressing, as it were, upon his senses. It was the congenial element of his moral being—the atmosphere in which his spirit was refreshed. There was no terror to *him* in the great and holy name; *he* felt no tumultuary agitation, because 'God had beset him behind and before, encompassing all his ways.' The recollection of this was rather a source of sacred and animated pleasure; it invested everything with a new property; it disclosed to him the spiritual essence that pervades the universe;

and thus gave him ever to feel as within the circle of the sublimest satisfactions."*

And so, my friends, do you seek Enoch's introduction to the living God. *Go* to him, as Enoch went, believing that he is, and that he is accessible.† And seek to get into the same just and realizing knowledge of him that Enoch got. He is revealed to you more amply, perhaps, than he was to Enoch. *Believe.* Believe that he is not afar off, but nigh. Believe that he is not hostile, but propitious. Believe that he is all that Jesus said—that he is all that Jesus was—and, believing this, *walk* with him. Admit him into your home, that he may hallow it. Admit him into your hourly occupations, that he may elevate and expedite them. Admit him into your happy moments, that he may enhance them; and into your hours of anguish, that his presence may tranquillize and transform them. Let his recollected presence be the brightness of every landscape—the zest of every pleasure—the energy for every undertaking—the refuge from every danger—the solace in every sorrow—the asylum of your hidden life, and the constant Sabbath of your soul. Learn—with all reverence for his greatness, but with equal reliance on his goodness—learn to make the eye that never slumbers the companion of your nights and mornings; and the ear that never wearies—make it the confidant of your weakness, your solicitude, your ecstasy, and woe. Learn to have not one life for God and another for the world; but let your earthly life

* Binney on Hebrews xi., pp. 89, 90   † Heb. xi. 6

be divinely directed and divinely quickened—let every footstep be a walk with God.

2. There was no prophet in Israel like unto Moses, whom the Lord knew face to face; and, like all the conspicuous characters of Scripture, Moses was a man of prayer. He, too, had been introduced into a peculiar acquaintance with the living God, and, from the memorable interview at the burning bush, there always rested on him an impress of that high fellowship to which he had been admitted. It was not only when the brightness of some recent interview lit up his countenance with new and painful glory; but, on his habitual look there lingered that blended benignity and majesty which, once seen in the aspect of Jehovah, its memorial might always be seen in himself. The Lord had heard Moses' prayer;* and, if he had not shown him all his glory, he had at least made all his goodness pass before him; and from that moment when, hidden in the mountain-cleft, the cloud swept over him, and the pulses of encircling power and sanctity thrilled through him, no conviction lodged deeper in Moses' mind, and no element of influence told more constantly on Moses' character, than the assurance that "the Lord is merciful and gracious, long-suffering, and abundant in goodness and truth." The secret of the Lord was with him; and surely it is important to know how one who knew the Lord's mind so well, and with whom the Lord so spake, face to face—how such a one was wont to pray. And I think you will notice these things in Moses' prayers:—(1., A *hopeful*

* Exodus xxxiii. 19.

ness which felt that no moment was too late, nor any depth of misery too profound, for prayer. When brought to a stand-still on the Red Sea shore—when almost poisoned by the waters of Marah—when like to be swallowed up by the fierceness of Amalek—it was all the same. Moses had instant recourse to the arm of Jehovah, and that arm brought salvation. And, in a case more daunting still—when successive sins had made the people outlaws from the covenant and its mercies—when they erected the golden calf— when Korah and his company rebelled—when Miriam was struck with leprosy—when the fire of God was sweeping through the camp—when the burning serpents were darting death and consternation on every side—these rapid plagues, the wickedness of the people, and their wild dismay, which would have made another leader 'faint," only made Moses pray. He recollected ' the Lord merciful and gracious, forgiving iniquity, transgression, and sin;" and, when other hearts were sinking, he still could " hope in God's mercy," and his hopeful prayers were ever procuring fresh forgiveness. (2.) And, besides this expectancy of mercy—this confidence of being heard—you may notice a holy *urgency* in Moses' prayers. How he pleads with God! How firm he takes his stand on the Divine perfections and the special promises, and with what security he argues from them! " Lord, why doth thy wrath wax hot against thy people, which thou hast brought forth out of the land of Egypt with great power, and with a mighty hand? Wherefore should the Egyptians speak and say 'For mischief did he bring them out, to slay them in the mountains, and to consume them from the face of the earth?' Turn from thy fierce wrath, and repent of this evil against thy people. Remember Abraham, Isaac, and Israel, thy servants, to whom thou swarest by thine own self, and saidst unto them, ' I will multiply your seed, as the stars of heaven, and all this land that I have spoken of will I give unto your seed and they shall inherit it for ever.* And that other time, when the Lord threatened to annihilate the murmuring people—" And now, I beseech thee, let the power of my Lord be great, according as thou hast spoken, saying, ' The Lord is long-suffering and of great mercy, forgiving iniquity and transgression, and by no means clearing the guilty.' Pardon, I beseech thee, the iniquity of this people, according unto the greatness of thy mercy, and as thou hast forgiven this people, from Egypt even until now.' And the Lord said, ' I have pardoned, according to thy word.' "†

From Moses, learn to pray and never faint. However awful the exigency, however near the destruction, and however abused past mercy may have been, still resort to him whose power is beyond all exigencies, and whose pity is more prompt than our repentance. And, from Moses, learn to glorify God, by pleading in prayer his perfections and his promises. That prayer will bring an absolute answer, which has for its foundation the Lord's absolute assurance; and, in the absence of a positive promise, that prayer will procure some mitigation or some mercy, which makes

* Exod. xxxii.   † Num. xiv. 17—20.

cordial mention of the Lord's goodness and loving-kindness. Remember the word unto thy servant, upon which thou hast caused me to hope.

3. Passing on to the "man after God's own heart," we find, of human models, the most perfect specimen of prayer. It is not so much the frequency of his devotional exercises, though these were seven times a day; nor the memorable returns which these prayers procured, for the prayers of Elijah and others may have brought about more miraculous results—may have drawn down, in the world's eye, more stupendous returns; but it is that DAVID was so signally a man of prayer, and that his prayers, in themselves are so pre-eminent. He prayed without ceasing, and with all prayer, in everything making known his requests, and in everything giving thanks. Taking possession of his new house, or retreating from it—on the eve of battle and in the flush of victory—among the sheep-cotes and in the mountain pass—on the tented field and in the trading town—in the shepherd's hut and on the monarch's throne—in the full height of spiritual joy and in the depths of guilty misery—we find him still the man of prayer. And these prayers have in them everything that enters into our idea of what prayer should be. David's was the darting eye that could catch upon the wing the fleetest of nature's phantoms and the swiftest flights of man's imaginings; and the divining eye that could detect the passion ere it mantled on Doeg's swarthy cheek, or read the cunning scheme ere it glanced from under Achithophel's polished brow. And his own soul was the well-tuned

harp on which, from the deep notes of dull and doubtful feeling up to the shrillest tones of ecstatic bliss or woe, the diapason sounded the full compass of all the emotions which this harp of thousand strings is able to express. And whilst his soul was thus susceptible and his eye thus quick, in his hand he held a poet's pen, and could transfer into equal words each intuition of his ranging eye and each aspiration of his yearning heart. And when you recollect that all this glowing fancy and earnest feeling and creative diction were the clothing of a spirit to which Jehovah was the chiefest joy—by which the living God was known and loved, adored and trusted—you can see how the Book of Psalms must ever be the best manual of devotion.

(1.) From David, learn in everything to pray. Learn to ask God's blessing on little things as well as great. There is nothing which it is right for us to do, but it is also right to ask that God would bless it; and, indeed, there is nothing so little but the frown of God can convert it into the most sad calamity, or his smile exalt it into a most memorable mercy; and there is nothing we can do but its complexion for weal or woe depends entirely on what the Lord will make it. It is said of Matthew Henry, that "no journey was undertaken, nor any subject or course of sermons entered upon; no book committed to the press, nor any trouble apprehended or felt, without a particular application to the mercy-seat for direction, assistance, and success."* And, on a studying day, he writes, "I forgot explicitly and

---

* Life, by Sir J B Williams, p. 211.

especially when I began to crave help of God, and the chariot-wheels drove accordingly."* It is recorded of Cornelius Winter, that he seldom opened a book, even on general subjects, without a moment's prayer.† The late Bishop Heber on each new incident of his history, or on the eve of any undertaking, used to compose a brief Latin prayer, imploring special help and guidance. No doubt such a prayer preceded the composition of his famous poem, "Palestine." At least, after it had gained the prize, and been read in the ears of applauding Oxford, when the assembly dismissed, the successful scholar could nowhere be found, till some one discovered him on his knees thanking God who had given him the power to produce that poem, and who had spared his parents to witness and share his joy.‡ A late physician of great celebrity used to ascribe much of his success to three maxims of his father, the last and best of which was, "Always pray for your patients."§

(2.) From David, learn to give thanks in everything. "Every furrow in the Book of Psalms is sown with seeds of thanksgiving."‖ Many of the Psalms are songs of vigorous and continuous praise: "O give thanks unto the Lord!" and others which begin with grief and confession and complaint, presently slide into gratitude. Praise is the believer's seemliest attire; and those have

* Tong's Life of Henry, p. 60.
† Jay's Life of Winter, p. 256.
‡ Life of Heber, quarto, vol. i., p. 33.
§ Memoir of James Hope, M.D., p. 51.
‖ Jeremy Taylor

been the most attractive Christians whose everyday adorning was the "garment of praise." It is mentioned of the famous Moravian, Count Zinzendorf, that " in his very aspect might be discerned the blessedness of a heart sprinkled from an evil conscience with the blood of the Lamb." " He looked for nothing but good from the Lord, in whom he delighted; and every subject of thankfulness, however inconsiderable it might seem to others, was important and interesting to him."* " I am surrounded with goodness, and scarcely a day passes over my head but I say, ' Were it not for an *ungrateful heart* I should be the happiest man alive ;' and *that* excepted, I neither expect nor wish to be happier in this world. My wife, my children, and myself in health; my friends kind; my soul at rest; and my labours successful. Who should not be content and thankful if I should not? O, my brother, help me to praise."†

(3.) From David, learn to delight in God, and so to view each scene in creation, and each event in providence, in God's own purest light. God was his chiefest joy, his sure and ascertained friend; and every scene was pleasant where God's presence was enjoyed, and every object interesting in which aught of God's glory could be seen. He felt Jehovah's tread in the shaking wilderness and the quivering forest. He saw Jehovah's chariot in the rolling cloud, the eddying tornado, and the wheeling water-spout. He beheld Jehovah's majestic flight on the wings of

* Life, pp. 508, 509.
† Fuller's Life of Pearce, p. 36

mighty winds and in the sweep of the careering clouds. He heard Jehovah's voice in the thunder-psalm and in ocean's echoing chime. He heard it, too, in the hum of leafy trees, and in the liquid music that trickled down the mountain's side. He recognised Jehovah's frown in the splitting rocks and smoking hills; and hailed Jehovah's smile in the melting tints of morning, in the laughing joy of harvest-fields, in the glancing roll of sun-steeped billows and the plunging gambols of leviathan as he played his ponderous frolics there.* Every touch of pathos or power passed away a heavenward melody from the Æolian harp of his devotional spirit; and, not content with these strains of constant adoration, on some occasions you can see him mustering all his being for some effort of ecstatic worship, and longing to flame away a holocaust of praise. Describing the change which came over his own feelings from the time that he knew God in Christ, President Edwards says, " The appearance of everything was altered; there seemed to be, as it were, a calm, sweet cast or appearance of Divine glory in almost everything. God's excellency, his wisdom, his purity and love, seemed to appear in everything; in the sun, and moon, and stars; in the clouds and blue sky; in the grass, flowers, trees; in the water and all nature, which used greatly to fix my mind. I often used to sit and view the moon for continuance; and in the day spent much time in viewing the clouds and sky, to behold the sweet glory of God in these things; in the mean time singing forth,

* See Psalms xxix., lxv., civ., cxlviii., &c.

with a low voice, my contemplations of the Creator and Redeemer. . . . My mind was greatly fixed on Divine things, almost perpetually in the contemplation of them. I oft walked alone in the woods and solitary places, for meditation, soliloquy, and prayer, and converse with God. . . . Prayer seemed to be natural to me, as the breath by which the inward burnings of my heart had vent."

4. And to take only one instance more,—" the man greatly beloved." DANIEL was a busy statesman. Darius had made him his chief minister. He had charge of the royal revenue, and was virtual ruler of the empire. But amidst all the cares of office he maintained his wonted custom of praying thrice a day.* For these prayers nothing was neglected. The administration of justice was not standing still; the public accounts did not run into confusion. There was no mutiny in the army, no rebellion in the provinces from any mismanagement of his. And though disappointed rivals were ready to found an impeachment on the slightest flaw, so wise and prompt and impartial was his procedure that they at last concluded, " We shall find no occasion against this Daniel, except we find it against him concerning the law of his God." He found leisure to rule the realm of Babylon, and leisure to pray three times a day. Some would say that he must have been a first-rate man of business to find so much time for prayer. It would be nearer the truth to say that it was his taking so much time to pray which made him so diligent and

* Dan. vi. 10

successful in business. It was from God that Daniel got his knowledge, his wisdom, and his skill. In the composure and serenity which these frequent approaches to God imparted to his spirit, as well as in the supernatural sagacity and forethought and power of arrangement which God gave in direct answer to his prayers, he had an infinite advantage over those men who, refusing to acknowledge God in their callings, vex themselves in vain, and who, when the fret and worry and sweltering of their jaded day is done, find that they have accomplished less, and that little far more painfully than their wiser brethren who took time to pray. The man must be busier than Daniel who has not time to pray, and wiser than Daniel who can do what Daniel did without prayer to help him. Daniel was in a place where prayer was eminently needful. He was in Babylon—a place of luxury and revelry—and from his position in society he was peculiarly exposed to the idolatrous and voluptuous temptations around him. It was difficult and ere long it was dangerous to maintain his singularity. But so far as there was any seduction in the mirth of that jovial city, prayer kept him separate; and so far as there was any danger in withholding countenance from its idol-orgies, prayer made him bold. Though the clash of the cymbal and the shouts of the dancers were coming in at the window, they did not disturb his devotion; and though he had not forgotten the king's decree and the lions' den, he did not close the lattice nor try to conceal his faith and his worship; and, secure alike from spiritual detriment and personal danger, the Lord hid his praying servant in the hollow of his hand.

Among the elegant forms of insect life, there is a little creature known to naturalists, which can gather round it a sufficiency of atmospheric air—and, so clothed upon, it descends into the bottom of the pool, and you may see the little diver moving about dry and at his ease, protected by his crystal vesture, though the water all around and above be stagnant and bitter. Prayer is such a protector—a transparent vesture, the world sees it not—but a real defence, it keeps out the world. By means of it the believer can gather so much of heaven's atmosphere around him, and with it descend into the putrid depths of this contaminating world, that for a season no evil will touch him; and he knows where to ascend for a new supply. Communion with God kept Daniel pure in Babylon. Nothing else can keep us safe in London. In secret of God's presence you might tread these giddy streets, and your eyes never view the vanity. You might pass theatres and taverns and never dream of entering in. You might get invitations to noisy routs and God-forgetting assemblies and have no heart to go. Golden images, public opinion with its lions' den, and fashion with its fiery furnace, would never disturb you. A man of prayer in this mart of nations, you could pass upon your way unseduced and undistracted, a Christian in Vanity Fair, a pilgrim in a paradise of fools, a true worshipper amidst idolaters, a Daniel in Babylon.

And so far as this is a world of distress and danger, prayer is the best defence. So Daniel found it in the den. So his three friends found it in the fiery furnace. And so you, my friends, will find it in the real or fancied perils of this mortal life. "The name of the Lord is a strong tower; the righteous runneth into it and is safe." An asylum ever open, the ejaculation of an instant will land you in it, and nothing is evil which befalls you there. By the omnipotent help which it at once secures, prayer is strength in weakness and courage in dismay. It is the buoy which rides the roaring flood, the asbestos-robe which defies the devouring flame. It is the tent in which frailty sleeps securely, and anguish forgets to moan. It is the shield on which the world and the wicked one expend their arts in vain. And when panic and temptation and agony all are over,—whether wafted by Sabbath zephyrs, or winged by scorching flames—whether guided by hymning angels, or dragged by raging lions—whether the starting-point be Patmos, or Jerusalem, or Smithfield, or Babylon, it is the chariot which conveys the departing spirit into a Saviour's arms.

LECTURE IX.

CONCLUSION.

"Praying always with all prayer and supplication in the Spirit."—EPHESIANS vi. 18.

Then what is prayer? Is it penance? Is it a part of that various punishment which God has inflicted on our sinful family? Is it so much holy drudgery to which every soul must force himself, under pain of incurring a severer penalty, or sinking at last into a deeper woe? Is it the irksome ordeal through which you are doomed to enter each successive day, and the moping and mournful *finale* with which you must close it up and leave it off? Is prayer the sackcloth which you must wear beneath the silk attire of daily joys,—the pebble which you must put into the sandals of daily business,—the preliminary thorn which you must break across or pluck away before you reach the downy pillow of this weary night's new slumber? Is prayer the cold fog which you must scatter over this world's bright landscape,—the memento mori with which you must sober down its merry melodies,—the Egyptian coffin at the banquet's close to lengthen every visage, and with quashed delight and bitter fancies to send each rueful guest away?

And yet, I am sure that it is in this sombre aspect that many look on prayer. Are you sure that this is not the aspect in which you yourself regard it? Is it not a task,—an exercise,—an endurance? Instead of engaging in it with that alacrity, or resorting to it with that avidity which would bespeak the privilege, do you not betake yourself to secret prayer with coldness and self-constraint, and feel, when the devotions of the family or sanctuary are ended, that it is a great comfort to have this other " duty " done?

What then is prayer?

1. It is communion with God. Oh! brethren, prayer is not an apostrophe to woods and wilds and waters. It is not a moan let fly upon the viewless winds, nor a bootless behest expended on a passing cloud. It is not a plaintive cry, directed to an empty echo, that can send back nothing but another cry. Prayer is a living heart that speaks in a living ear,—the ear of the living God. It matters not where the worshipper is,—on a dreary shore; in a noisome dungeon; amidst the filth and ferocity of brutal savages, or the frivolity and atheism of hollow hearted worldlings; surrounded by the whirr and clash and roaring dissonance of the heaving factory, or toiling in the depths of the lamp-lit mine,—the man of prayer need never feel the withering pangs of loneliness. Wherever you are the Lord is there, and it only needs prayer to bring Himself and you together. Recollect him, and he is beside your path; resort to him, and he lays his hand upon you. And who is this ever-present Help,—this never-distant Friend? Words

cannot tell. The Incarnate "Word" *did* tell, but few could comprehend, and as few could credit.* If you imagine the tenderest affection of your most anxious Friend; the mildest condescension and readiest sympathy of your most appreciating and considerate Friend; and if you add to this a goodness and a wisdom, such as you never saw in the best and wisest of your friends; and if you do not merge but multiply all this wisdom, all this goodness, and all this kindness towards you by infinity, so as to give this tender and constant Friend infinite knowledge to watch over you, infinite forethought to provide for you, and infinite resources to relieve or enrich you; if you did not fully realize who the hearer and answerer of prayer is, you would, at least, be a step beyond that unknown God, whom many ignorantly and joylessly worship. In prayer you do not address a general law or a first principle, but you address a living person. You do not commune with eternity, or with infinite space, but you commune with the Father of eternity,— with Him "who fills the highest heavens, and who also dwells in the lowliest hearts." You do not hold converse with abstract goodness, but with the God and Father of our Lord Jesus Christ; with God in Christ; with Him whose express image Jesus is; with Jesus himself; with your Friend within the veil; with your Father who is in heaven.

And is there in this aught that should prove repulsive or heart-chilling? Is Christ so altered from what he was, that you needs must depre-

John i. 5, 18.

cate his presence; or are you so earthly, so sensual, so sin-saturated, that though he were talking with you by the way your bosom could not burn? The Saviour and yourself; is there so little friendship between you? is he so little a reality that days pass without adverting to him? or is he so little loved that you rather deprecate than desire his coming? Have you found so little that is engaging in him that you wonder how people who loved one another dearly, loved this Saviour more? Or is the whole such a phantom,—to your feelings such a nonentity,—that you cannot comprehend how any one should have such delight in God as to cry out in desire of his more conscious presence, "O God, thou art my God; early will I seek thee: my soul thirsteth for thee, my flesh longeth for thee in a dry and thirsty land. My soul shall be satisfied as with marrow and fatness, when I remember thee upon my bed, and meditate on thee in the night-watches."

Yes, brethren, whatever you may fancy—or rather, whatever you may forget—the Lord liveth. There may be objects which fascinate all your soul, and bind in welcome fetters all your faculties; but hidden from your view there is an object, did you catch one glimpse of him, fit to deaden the deliciousness of every lesser joy, and darken the glare of every lesser glory. There may be friends deep-seated in your soul, but there is yet one friend, whom could you but discover, he would make you another man—he would give your life a new nobility, your character a new sanctity. He would give yourself a new existence in giving himself to you, and would give society a new manner of person in giving you to it. And with this glorious personage, and withal most gracious friend, it is possible to keep up an intercourse to which the most rapid communication and the closest converse of earth supply not the equivalent. The twinkling thought—the uplifted eye—the secret groan—will bring him in an instant—will bring him in all the brightness of his countenance through the midnight gloom—in all the promptitude of his interposition through the thickest dangers—in all the abundance of his strength into the fading flesh—and in all the sweetness of his sympathy and assurance of his death-destroying might into the failing heart. And this communion, closer and more complete than that of any creature with another—for dearest friend can only give his thoughts, and desires, and feelings—he cannot impart himself; but in regard to the praying soul and this divine communion, we read of its being " filled with all the fulness of God."

2. Prayer is peace and joy. Two things constitute the believer's peculiarity and make him differ from the rest of men—just as two things constitute the sinner's peculiarity, and make him differ from the rest of God's creatures. The two things which form the Christless sinner's peculiar misery, are *guilt* and *vacancy*—a gloom above him and a void within him. A gloom above him—for he has no confidence in God—he has no hopeful and confiding feeling heavenwards—no firm reliance on a reconciled God, and no smiling vista through a pierced and heaven-open-

ing sepulchre. A sense of sin—in shadowy hauntings or in severe and burning incubus—is lowering over his conscience, and whether it merely mar his occasional joy, or convert his days into habitual misery, this guilt, this conscience of sin is a serious abatement on the zest of existence—a mournful deduction from the total of earthly joy. It makes the unpardoned sinner's walk very different from the seraph's limpid flight, who only knows guilt by distant report, and very different from the newly-pardoned sinner's lightened gaiety, who only knows it by remembrance—breaking his daily bread in the sprightliness of a vanished fear, and eating it with the relish of a conscious innocency. But not only is there a gloom above the Christless sinner—a brooding guilt, and an impending danger—but there is a void within him. God did not create man at first with that burden on his conscience, and neither did he create him with this aching gap in his bosom. Or rather, we should say the all-wise Creator has implanted no craving in any of his creatures, without having provided some counterpart object. When that object is attained, the creature is content. The craving subsides in quiet enjoyment and complacency. It is happy and wants no more. The ox is at home in his rich pasture, and sends no wistful thought beyond it; and so is the insect which "expands and shuts its wings in silent ecstasy" on the edge of the sunny flower. But it is far otherwise with the roaming soul of the Christless sinner. There is no flower of earthly growth in whose nectar bathing he can finally forget his poverty—no green pastures of time-bounded blessedness in whose amplitudes he can so lose himself that misery shall find him no more. Wide as is his range, his anxious eye sees too well its weary limits, and sweet as the honeyed petals are, he perceives them dying as he drinks. Oh! this fugacity of all that is pleasant—this scanty measure and momentary duration of earthly delights was never meant to satiate the soul of man—this never is the counterpart which the bountiful Jehovah created for the yearning avidity of an immortal spirit. Cast into the mighty gulf of man's craving soul, a house-full of friendship, a ship's freight of wealth and dainty delights, a world-load of wondrous objects and lovely scenes,—the deep-sounding abyss will ever echo, " Give, give;" and though you could tumble the world itself into the heart of man, you could not prevent it from collapsing in disappointment, and dying vacant and dreary at last.

There is only one object so mighty as truly to content this capacious desire—only one ultimatum so conclusive that when the soul has reached it, it has nothing more to do than rest it and rejoice. That object is the living God himself, that ultimatum is the All-sufficient Jehovah. The Gospel meets the two desiderata of our uneasy and anxious humanity by offering a free pardon and an infinite and eternal possession. The affrighted and apprehensive soul finds peace where it finds forgiveness; and the yearning, discontented soul finds joy where it finds a never-dying, all-sufficient friend. It finds them both where it finds Immanuel. The gloom vanishes and the void is filled—the query of existence is answered, and the problem of blessedness solved when the soul ascertains what Jesus really is, and in a Saviour-God discovers its Beloved and its Friend.

Now the peace and joy of conversion it is one great use of prayer to reproduce and perpetuate. It brings the soul into the presence of that Saviour, whom in the day of salvation it found, and renewing the intercourse, it renews the joy. When prayer is what it ought to be—when it is earnest and realizing—it gives the believer fellowship with the Father, and with his Son Jesus Christ. It brings him in contact with those perfections of the Godhead which may at the moment be chiefly revealed to his view: and in the pavilion of prayer—beneath the canopy of the sure atonement, and on the safe standing-point of acceptance—the soul surveys the God of majesty, or surrenders itself to the God of grace—hearkens to his dreadful voice in the thundering power of startling providences, or melts in sweet amazement beneath the full flood of his marvellous mercies—but from every aspect of awful solemnity or benignant endearment, the assuring thought comes home, "And this God is our own God for ever." And perhaps there is no influence so abidingly tranquillizing—so permanently hallowing and heart-assuring, as this high communion with the great All in All. The pleasures of sin will look paltry, and sin itself disgusting to eyes which have just been gazing on the fountain of light. The tossings of time—mountains of prosperity rooted up, and pinnacles of fortune flung into the roaring sea—will look trivial matters to one who has eyed them in their mote-like distance from beneath the sapphire throne. And even the groans of mortality and the wailings of the sepulchre will come diluted and transformed to ears resounding with golden harmonies from the holy place of the Most High.

3. Prayer is the only means of importing to earth blessings not native to it. There are many commodities not of English growth, which ships and wealth and enterprise can fetch from foreign shores. But there are some things which no wealth can purchase, which no enterprise can compass, and with which no ship that ever rode the seas came freighted. Where is the emporium to which you can resort and order so much happiness? Where is the ship that ever brought home a cargo of heart-comfort?—a consignment of good consciences?—a freight of strength for the feeble, and joy for the wretched, and peace for the dying? But what no vessel ever fetched from the Indies, prayer has often fetched from heaven. Our earth is insulated. It is clean cut off from all intercourse with the most adjacent worlds. But even though the nearest world were peopled by holy and happy beings, and though they could cross the great gulf that severs them from us, they could accomplish little for us. They could not bind up bleeding hearts—they could not wash stains from guilty souls—they could not infuse their own felicity into gaunt and joyless hearts, and they could not transport their own sweet atmosphere so as to heal the miasma of a polluted

place, or the misery of a wretched home. But what they cannot do, the Lord himself can do. Prayer is not a message to the moon. It is not a cry for help to the sun, or to the stars in their courses. It is a petition addressed to Him who made the sun and moon and stars. It is recourse to the ever-present and all-sufficient God. It is frailty fleeing to omnipotence. It is misery at the door of mercy. It is worm Jacob at the ladder's foot, and that ladder's top in heaven. It is the dying thief beside a dying Saviour, and the same Paradise already open for them both. The mercy-seat is the ark of the covenant opened, and the legend over it, " Ask, and it shall be given thee." And prayer is just the exploring eye and the believing hand selecting from the " unsearchable riches of Christ" the sweetest mercies and the costliest gifts. Jacob compared Joseph his son to a fruitful tree inside of a lofty fence ;* but though he grew in a " garden enclosed," his growth was so luxuriant that his branches ran over the wall, and the wandering Ishmaelites, and the hungry passengers shot their arrows and flung their missiles at the laden boughs, and caught up such clusters as fell outside the fence. The tree of life grows now in such a garden. There is now an enclosure round it, but the branches run over the wall. High over our heads we may perceive the bending boughs, and such fragrant fruits as " peace of conscience, joy in the Holy Ghost, assurance of God's love," " gentleness, goodness, faith, meekness, temperance"—and prayer is the arrow

* Gen. xlix. 22, 23, with Harmer's explanation.

which detaches these from the bough—the missile which brings these far-off fruits, these lofty clusters, down to the dusty path, and the weary traveller's feet. Happy he whose believing prayer is "like Jonathan's bow, which never came empty back."*

4. Prayer confers the largest power of doing good to others. " What am I to do with other people's sorrows?" The finest and the gentlest spirits are often the most heavily burdened. Many a one feels that he could pass right easily through the world if he had no griefs to carry but his own. He feels that his sensitive system is just a contrivance for catching up other men's calamities,—an apparatus on which every body fastens his own peculiar vexation—his family their's—his neighbours their's—till at last he moves about the burden-bearer of a groaning world. But after he has got himself thus charged and loaded, he knows not what to do, for he cannot alleviate the twentieth portion of the ills he knows. He cannot heal all the wounds and mitigate all the poverty of which he is the mourning witness. He cannot minister to all the minds diseased, all the aching hearts and wounded spirits whose confidant he is; and in the anguish of his own tortured sympathies he is sometimes tempted to turn these sympathies outside in, and feel for his fellow-men no more. "What then shall I do with other people's sorrows?" The Christian feels that he has no right to be his own little all-in-all. He feels that he dares not invert the example of his Master, who was a man of

* Gurnall

sorrows very much because a man of sympathies. He remembers of whom it is said, "Surely he hath borne our griefs and carried our sorrows;" and this reminds him what to do with the perplexities and disappointments and distresses of his brethren. He takes them to the Throne of Grace. He deposits them in the ear of the Great High Priest. He urges them on the notice of one who can be touched with a feeling of infirmity, and who is able to succour them that are tempted. And in this way a believer who is tender-hearted enough to feel for his brethren, and who is so much a man of prayer as to carry to the mercy-seat those matters that are too hard and those griefs that are too heavy for himself, may be a greater benefactor to his afflicted friends than an Achitophel who has nothing but sage counsel, or a Joab who has nothing but a stout arm to help them—than a man of fortune who can give nothing but his money, or a man of feeling who has nothing but his tears. The Christian has his near relations and personal friends. Parents and children, brothers and sisters, husbands and wives, —God has bound them very closely together, and made it impossible for the joy of one to be full if another's joy is incomplete. Besides these there are friends not of one's house—kindred spirits whom God, in creating, or the Spirit of God, in new-creating, has made congenial with your own —those to whom you are drawn by the affnity of identical tastes, or by the discovery of those mental gifts and spiritual graces, which cannot be hid, and which cannot be seen without attracting you. Now one way to sanctify such friendships is to make them the materials and the incentives of prayer. For example, there may be seasons of spiritual languor when you have little heart to pray. The Throne of Grace seems distant or uninviting. A deep sloth has seized the inner man. You are not inclined to ask any blessing for yourself. You are too carnal to confess any sin, and too sullen to acknowledge any mercy—perhaps so earthly or atheistical that you do not pant—nay, do not breathe after God, the living God. At such a season of deadness you will sometimes find that you can pray for others when you cannot for yourself.* Do even so. Make your solicitude for them a motive for prayer Begin by laying their wants before the Lord, and you will soon find out your own. Come in their company, and you may soon find yourself left alone with God. This is not to desecrate prayer, but to consecrate friendship. It exalts and purifies affection, and by making it friendship in the Lord, makes it more lasting now, and more likely to be renewed hereafter.

And lastly, Intercession sanctifies the believer's relation to the Church. "Our Father" makes all of us who are in Christ one family. But this, too, is oft forgotten. There is little family love amongst us yet—little instinctive affection resulting from our common adoption into the circle of God's dear children—little of that affection towards one another which our elder brother feels towards very one—little outgoing of sympathy because one Comforter fills us all. If the family relation of the household of

---

* Sheppard's Thoughts on Private Devotion

faith be ever realized, it is in social or intercessory prayer. Abba, Father—my Father truly, because Father of my Lord Jesus Christ; but, if so, Father of many more—Father of the whole believing family—" Our Father, which art in heaven." And so the circle widens, till, starting from the individual, or his own little band of immediate brotherhood, it includes all whom the arms of Immanuel enclose. One who was much given to intercessory prayer writes thus to a Christian friend:—" I beseech you to seek earnestly the communion of saints. This is the only progress I have made in the divine life. I have received, as a most precious and unmerited gift, the power of feeling the things of the flock of Christ as if they were my own. You cannot imagine the happiness of this feeling. I dedicate an hour every evening to prayer, and principally to intercession. I generally begin with the thanks due to God for having made himself known to us as our Father, for all that he has done for every one of his sheep on that day. It is impossible for me to tell you the great delight of thus mixing myself up with the people of Christ, and of considering their benefits as my own. The thought which transports me the most, is that of how many souls have been, perhaps, this day joined to the Church! how many succoured under temptation! how many recovered from their backslidings! how many filled with consolation! how many transported by death into the bosom of Christ! I then try to pray for that sweet ' we,' and to think of the necessities of my Christian friends. Besides, I have a list of unconverted persons, for whom I wish to pray."* And, if there were more of this spirit, how it would alter the tone of Christians to one another! Instead of being so censorious and uncharitable, it would make us feel, " Am I not my brother's keeper ?" Instead of a fault-finding, it would make us a fault-forgiving and a fault-healing Church. It would make us suffer with the suffering members, and exult with the rejoicing. It would make us like that high-souled apostle who had " continual heaviness " for his unconverted kindred, and who yet never wanted topics of consolation ; remembering without ceasing in his prayers his believing brethren, with their work of faith, and labour of love, and patience of hope.

* " Memoir of Miss M. J Graham," second edition, pp. 375, 376

www.ingramcontent.com/pod-product-compliance
Lightning Source LLC
Chambersburg PA
CBHW030300170426
43202CB00009B/814